Teachers leading inquiry for school problem solving

Teachers leading inquiry for school problem solving

Edited by
Rebecca Jesson, Aaron Wilson,
Stuart McNaughton, and Mei Lai

NZCER PRESS

NZCER PRESS
New Zealand Council for Educational Research
PO Box 3237
Wellington
New Zealand

www.nzcer.org.nz

© Authors 2017

ISBN 978-1-98-854211-9

No part of the publication may be copied, stored, or communicated
in any form by any means (paper or digital), including recording
or storing in an electronic retrieval system, without the written
permission of the publisher.
Education institutions that hold a current licence with Copyright
Licensing New Zealand may copy from this book in strict accordance
with the terms of the CLNZ Licence.

A catalogue record for this book is available from the National Library
of New Zealand.

Designed by Smartwork Creative Ltd

Dedication

We dedicate this book to Sir John Graham who as a Trustee of the Woolf Fisher Trust was a staunch advocate for the Lead Teacher Scholarship. All the students and their supervisors in this book benefitted enormously from Sir John's encouragement and challenging but always constructive critique.

Kua hinga te tōtara i te wao nui a Tāne
The tōtara has fallen in the forest of Tāne

Acknowledgements

The studies in this book were generously funded by the Woolf Fisher Trust. The purpose of the Scholarships was to enable outstanding teachers from Auckland and Northland schools to be released from school duties to undertake a research master's degree involving training at the Woolf Fisher Research Centre in school-based research and development methods. The editors and contributors wish to give particular thanks to the Trustees.

The editors are also very grateful to Victoria Cockle for her excellent copyediting of the manuscript.

Contents

INTRODUCTION

The Lead Teacher Master's Research Scholarship Programme — 1
Rebecca Jesson and Aaron Wilson

Solving pressing challenges: The role of a Lead Teacher — 4
Stuart McNaughton

PART 1 INQUIRING INTO PATTERNS OF STUDENT LEARNING — 9
Aaron Wilson and Rebecca Jesson

Chapter 1 Pacific girls' perceptions of the enablers and barriers in Level 3 NCEA English: A little talanoa goes a long way — 13
Carol Jarrett

Chapter 2 Overcoming a plateau in mathematics learning — 18
Trish Holster

Chapter 3 Does Samoan Bilingual education make a difference? — 22
Jacqui Tutavake

Chapter 4 Patterns of literacy progress, achievement, and the development of self-regulating young readers in a high-decile school — 25
Liz Lapish

PART 2 INQUIRING INTO TEACHING AND OPPORTUNITIES TO LEARN — 29
Aaron Wilson

Chapter 5 Patterns of vocabulary instruction in Years 1–3 following professional development — 35
Caroline Chawke

Chapter 6 Effective academic counselling for Māori students in a Northland high school — 39
Rochelle Telfer

Chapter 7 Facets of the gemstone: Effective teaching for Pasifika students in Level 2 English — 44
Richard Watkinson

Chapter 8 Students speak about 'Student Speak': Student perceptions of formative e-assessment results — 49
Susan Smith

Chapter 9 Barriers and enablers to students' self-management in BYOD environments — 52
Kerry Boyde-Preece

Chapter 10 Implementation of Academic Counselling by tutor teachers at a low-decile secondary school — 55
Lynne Savage

PART 3 INQUIRING INTO TEACHERS' PROFESSIONAL LEARNING — 59
Mei Lai

Chapter 11 **Professional Learning Communities: Properties of effective collaborative inquiry in a primary school setting** — 63
Catherine Biggs

Chapter 12 **Does Reading Recovery training change the way teachers interact with students in guided reading?** — 66
Heather Hardy

Chapter 13 **How teacher–leaders make sense of what they learn when they are involved in multiple inquiries** — 70
Gina Hemmingsen

Chapter 14 **Features of success: A study of an effective teaching community** — 73
Kim Henry with Aaron Wilson

PART 4 FAMILIES AND PARTNERSHIPS — 77
Rebecca Jesson

Chapter 15 **Empowering parents and improving reading: Investigating an intervention for adolescent readers** — 83
David Taylor

Chapter 16 **Developing a home–school partnership to support Year 9 students in mathematics** — 87
Sam McNaughton

Chapter 17 **Understanding parents' perspectives of the IEP process** — 92
Sharon Fuemana

References — 96

About the authors — 101

Introduction

The Lead Teacher Master's Research Scholarship Programme

Rebecca Jesson and Aaron Wilson

While 'teaching as inquiry' is a key precept of the *New Zealand Curriculum* (Ministry of Education, 2007a), the focus on shared inquiry within schools to effect educational improvement requires an advanced combination of analytical skills and sophisticated content knowledge. The Woolf Fisher Lead Teacher Master's Scholarship programme ran for 5 years from 2011–15 and provided the opportunity for highly talented teachers to be released from their school for a year to develop research and collective problem-solving skills while addressing a persistent educational challenge facing their school. During that time, leaders from schools worked for a year with the team at Woolf Fisher Research Centre to develop detailed analyses of key aspects of learning, teaching, and schooling processes. As part of that investigation, lead teachers developed research skills, produced detailed analyses of complex problems, and contributed to understanding theoretical as well as applied issues. Each of the studies represented here adds to understandings about key parts of the school-wide inquiry process to find solutions and innovate in individual schools.

At the Woolf Fisher Research Centre, we have based our work around a cycle of inquiry that we call the Learning Schools Model (LSM). Researchers at the Centre use the model as a way of working with schools in Research–Practice Partnerships. As a collaborator we work with groups of schools to understand the relationships between the patterns of student learning and patterns of teaching within a cluster. The approach employs design-based research situated in a real educational context, to design and test hypotheses about the relationships between patterns of teaching and patterns of learning. The approach requires multiple cycles of data collection, analysis, and feedback. These data are used by both researchers and schools as a basis to design more effective instruction. The process is formative, leading to the redesign of teaching practices predicted to address the learning needs.

The Woolf Fisher Lead Teachers Research Scholarships programme built on the knowledge gained through the Learning Schools Model research projects about effective processes for inquiry by school leaders at school level (e.g., McNaughton, Lai, Jesson & Wilson, 2013). It provided an apprenticeship for teachers to develop research capability through participation in a research-based master's degree. Teachers developed their skills and expertise in research and development, and applied processes of inquiry and site-based problem solving to work within their schools.

The programme showed that Lead Teachers can build schools' capacity to focus systematically on their own improvement needs. In partnership with their supervisors, the lead teachers learned to identify strengths and weaknesses in student learning and educational provision through collecting, interpreting, and using evidence from their schools. Teachers developed a systematic approach to understanding student learning, teaching, and teacher knowledge building, enabling them to adapt to different students' and teachers' backgrounds and needs, and to test innovations.

Major components investigated through their research work in schools included:

1. developing specific hypotheses through profiles of teaching and learning
2. ongoing learning through use of local evidence (teaching and learning) to fine-tune specific components of their educational provision
3. professional learning to promote systematic inquiry to solve achievement problems
4. working with whānau to support students' learning.

For each of the studies in this book, the Lead Teachers designed and implemented a specific study based on the specific educational issue and context. An underlying assumption of all the projects was that they used local evidence and were tailored to the local context. So, the approach designed for a specific context would need significant modification in other contexts. However, each of the studies highlights a number of key *processes* that were crucial to the Lead Teachers' endeavours. We realise that not all teachers doing valuable inquiry about persistent issues in their context will want or need to be as in-depth and rigorous in their investigations as the Lead Teachers needed to be for formal qualifications. We do hope, though, that their experiences might provide a springboard and useful ideas for other Lead Teachers, investigating a stubborn, hard-to-change issue in other contexts.

Solving pressing challenges: The role of a Lead Teacher

Stuart McNaughton

Four pressing challenges face New Zealand educators as we work to develop even more equitable and excellent educational systems. They are not about teaching quality in the sense of discovering more about effective pedagogy, or discovering the most effective programmes. They are not about more extensive critique of what we know are risks in policy developments such as types of assessments. The four challenges are each about learning from what we do well to improve our system overall.

These four challenges are:

1. sustaining in classrooms and schools what we do effectively
2. applying that effectiveness to new classrooms and schools
3. using the variability in how different students, teachers, and schools do things to identify innovation on the one hand and to increase consistency of effective practice on the other
4. building capability of teachers, rather than relying on prescription or programme specification.

These are all related.

Take variability first. Variability is a fundamental feature of everything we do in education. Variability can be seen at various levels. At the most general level, there is variability between and within countries at a point in time as shown in international comparisons, and in countries over time. For example, the amount of our variance in achievement that is related to children's backgrounds (socio-economic status) is higher than the OECD average and, until the most recent PISA study, was getting higher.

The studies in this book are concerned with the variability in students' outcomes and experiences and variability in teaching. This variability is apparent on just about any metric we wanted to choose. One example is that at least some of the variability in how much academic learning takes place over summer is attributable to what teachers do at the end of the school year and at the beginning of the new school year, and individual teachers vary tremendously (Jesson, McNaughton & Kolose, 2014). Other examples can be found in the evaluations of programmes in New Zealand. Projects such as The Secondary Literacy Project (Wilson & McNaughton, 2013) or Te Kotahitanga (Bishop, Berryman & Wearmouth, 2014) often end with marked variability between schools in terms of improvements in student outcomes, related to what was actually done and how, even though the schools have been engaged in the same project over a number of years. In this book, there are many examples of Lead Teachers using some aspect of variability to understand what works for whom, and why, in their educational context.

What does that variability represent? It certainly represents gradations of effectiveness and, at the extreme positive end of an achievement distribution, the outliers are excellent and innovative teachers and schools. The lack of greater consistency means either we haven't been prescriptive enough about the practices that are needed, or that we need to pay more attention to building the capability of teachers through developing their knowledge and skills. Both of these are useful explanations for the lack of consistency and signal the appropriate directions to take, although just what the balance between these might be depends on the nature of being effective and the context for being effective.

The issues of sustainability and scaling are related to this issue of variability. In order to sustain an aspect of our teaching or a programme we need to have very good evidence for how the effective teaching works on the ground in local contexts, and what doesn't work well. We need evidence for what elements need to be closely followed or adapted to new and potentially very different circumstances as these change, such as changes in teachers, students, and communities, to say nothing of curricula and technology changes over time. Similarly, in order to take our effective teaching to scale we need to have very robust evidence of what works, for whom, under what conditions, and across potentially very different circumstance of schools (Bryk, Gomez, Grunow, & LeMahieu, 2015). These different conditions include the identities and background of students, and the cultural, linguistic, and educational resources within and between schools and their communities.

For 5 years from 2011, with funding from the Woolf Fisher Trust, The Woolf Fisher Research Centre[1] set out to test one component of what we theorised was needed to meet these four challenges. We had spent several years in school improvement studies and large-scale interventions. We had confronted and had tentative solutions for the four challenges. For example, we knew that 'profiling' the problem using various sources of evidence was a key component and we knew that well-structured and content-rich discussions of these data were needed. In these and other components the role of an expert leader who could help define the problem through evidence, who could help lead data discussions and the testing and retesting, was crucial. This role, which we as researchers had largely carried out with leaders within the schools, required quite specific and complex skills, ranging from data analysis, through hypothesis testing, through to social and emotional skills for working with colleagues and communities.

We set out to test whether we could develop these skills in others. Each year we spent the whole year working with a specially selected cohort of highly talented teachers who were completing their master's research thesis. They were to solve or at least develop a testable explanation for an achievement or learning 'problem' in their school. The problem could be an innovative or known area of effectiveness, as much

---

1   www.education.auckland.ac.nz/en/about/research/wfrc.html

as a difficulty or an area of ineffectiveness. In either case the problem was to understand and test an explanation for the effectiveness/ineffectiveness as a means to being able to sustain or scale effectiveness, be more consistently effective, and build capability. In the course of the year they developed skills for:

1. collecting and using evidence to identify (and clarify) the achievement problem, and in the process rejecting unlikely explanations
2. planning a collaborative intervention from a sound knowledge base with staff in the school to address the problem
3. to evaluate the impact of the intervention where appropriate; and
4. to write this up as a submitted thesis.

What did we learn from this test? In essence this book provides part of the evidence. The case studies in this book highlight the role of each of these Lead Teachers for solving educational problems. They also illustrate the skills developed in carrying out these roles: skills possibly not traditionally thought of as educational or teaching traits, but essential for in-school problem solving; for example in identifying the problem, finding out in detail about the manifestations of that problem, investigating variability associated with it, checking assumptions, and developing and testing hypotheses.

The idea was a forerunner to the major reform of 'Investing in Educational Success' developed by the New Zealand government in 2014. Similar roles came to be called Within and Across School Lead Teachers and were to function in the newly forming Communities of Learning | Kāhui Ako. They have been designed to work with other teachers to help identify and respond to challenges in practice, and to learn with and from their colleagues in cycles of inquiry and improvement.[2] The processes of inquiry used by the Lead Teachers in this book will be highly useful examples for those who are leading inquiry in Kāhui Ako.

---

2 https://education.govt.nz/communities-of-learning/leadership-and-governance

PART 1 INQUIRING INTO PATTERNS OF STUDENT LEARNING

Aaron Wilson and Rebecca Jesson

Each of the studies in this section forms an inquiry into student achievement issues. In most cases, the inquiries were sparked by a mismatch between what was wanted for the students and what was being achieved, with school leaders and teachers who were at a loss to explain the patterns that they were seeing. In Carol's case, why did it seem that students, who had been successful in English all the way through their schooling, now struggle with NCEA Level 3? For Liz, why would students who enter school with high emergent literacy skills not make more progress? For Trish, why might students be 'plateauing' at Stage 5 of the numeracy progressions? Jacqui's study was a slight exception. For her, the inquiry was sparked by a need to investigate whether the recently established bilingual unit was making the desired impact for their learners.

Because learning is so crucial to schools, in each of the studies, the Lead Teachers sought to detail a rich picture of student learning, in a systematic way, with a high degree of specificity. Each needed to identify, check, prioritise, and investigate learning, and so each needed to understand what worked (or didn't) for whom, and under what conditions. Although all the studies in this section focused on student learning, none focused exclusively on achievement outcomes. Wider outcomes for students were also valued; for example, culture (Carol, Jacqui), languages (Jacqui), relationships (Carol), and self-regulation (Liz). Outcomes for teachers and families were also valued; for example, teacher knowledge (Trish, Liz) and home–school connections (Jacqui).

To gain a detailed picture of students' learning, the Lead Teachers needed to investigate students' achievement levels and their progress and to seek a level of detail to unmask patterns. Knowing about students' achievement levels at a single point in time as well as their progress over multiple points of time is needed if we are to gain a rich picture of their learning. Clearly, the most desirable situation is for students to have high levels of achievement and to be making high rates of progress, whereas having low levels of achievement and low rates of progress is the least desirable situation. It is vital that we investigate both achievement and progress because the implications for students and teachers of low levels / high progress rates, for example, are very different from high levels / low progress rates. The latter is what Liz found. Students at her school seemed to be doing well with more students at or above the National Standards than other schools. However, when she examined progress as well as achievement, she identified that progress rates were much lower than expected. It seemed to her that the 'high on average' achievement had actually masked a problem of progress.

Lead Teachers used different approaches to investigate students' achievement and progress. In the earliest stages of their inquiry most used some form of cross-sectional data. The assumption of cross-sectional analyses is that different cohorts of students in a particular school are fairly similar from year to year. In many high schools we would predict the mean achievement of Year 9 students at the beginning of Term 1 in 2016 to be pretty close to that of a new cohort of Year 9 students at the same time of year in 2017. That being the case, we can estimate the amount of progress students make by comparing the levels of Year 9 students with those in Year 10 in the same year. When cohorts are fairly large, and there have not been major changes in school or student factors, such as professional development or demographics, cross-sectional analyses can give a useful snapshot of patterns. For several of the Lead Teachers, including Carol, Liz, and Trish, preliminary analysis of cross-sectional data was what had first alerted them to problematic patterns in student achievement in the first place.

A limitation of cross-sectional analyses of course is that internal and external factors mean different cohorts of students can be quite different from one another. For this reason, most of the Lead Teachers went on to use longitudinal analyses whereby they matched individual students' data over time. This is a complicated and laborious process but it allowed the Lead Teachers to be much more accurate and precise in their judgements about progress. Longitudinal analyses enabled Carol, for example, to identify two key patterns. First, high-achieving Pacific girls tended to have lower grades in Level 3 NCEA English than Level 2, whereas the pattern was opposite for girls from other backgrounds. Secondly, Pacific girls' progress was more varied (or volatile, as Carol called it) than other girls'; their Level 2 results were not as reliable a predictor of Level 3 results. The 'volatility' could not have been identified without longitudinal matching of individual students' Level 2 and Level 3 grades. Repeating the analysis for different cohorts of students, and finding the same patterns, meant Carol could be more confident that the issues were not restricted to a single cohort. In Jacqui's study, matching the students over 3 full years allowed her to notice improvements for bilingual students in their reading progress over summer, not equalled by their peers in mainstream classes.

Variability between students (comparison between groups) and in the same students over time (comparison between time points) formed the basis for all of the inquiries. Inquiring into levels required looked at patterns of attainment at a specific point in time; looking for specific strengths and gaps; behaviours, practices, skills in different contexts; and attitudes and beliefs. Inquiring into progress meant matching individual students' data over time, sometimes over years (Jacqui). This detailed picture was required so that the Lead Teachers could 'check' perceptions (Carol), 'check' that the problem they identified was a real problem (Liz), and drill down into which aspects of learning were the most problematic (Trish) or were most advantageous (Jacqui).

The use of mixed methods in the studies allowed the Lead Teachers to come at an inquiry in different ways, garnering a multi-dimensional view on the learning. Methods drawn on by scholars included both quantitative analyses of achievement results, and qualitative analyses of interviews, artefacts (e.g. work samples or planning documents), or observations. Each of the Lead Teachers used achievement data to find the patterns, but each also used a qualitative method to understand the patterns. Liz, for example, observed the children in reading groups, Carol talked with students throughout their Year 13 year, Trish analysed teachers' planning and assessment, talked with teachers, as well as interviewing the students, and Jacqui interviewed teachers and family members. These insights provided valuable evidence, but none of the methods was enough by itself. Instead, the mixture of evidence helped the scholars develop a detailed picture of the issue, from different angles. While the designs differed, in many cases the Lead Teachers divided their studies into phases, with an initial phase to describe the patterns, and a later phase to seek understanding of them. In this way, the studies often employed a *mixed methods, sequential, explanatory* design.

Finally, each of the scholars demonstrated the need to be cautious in their interpretations. Sometimes the studies were restricted to looking at quite small numbers. In these cases the Lead Teachers needed to beware of making too much of one source of data. Instead, each considered the data as only part of the picture, building up the weight of evidence by drawing from different sources, or cutting the data in different ways, or bringing multiple data sources together. In each case, the convergence of evidence allowed the Lead Teacher to draw tentative conclusions which could be supported by evidence, or to develop hypotheses which could be tested through collection of new evidence.

Chapter 1 Pacific girls' perceptions of the enablers and barriers in Level 3 NCEA English: A little talanoa goes a long way

Carol Jarrett

The study arose from a perception among teachers in the school that Pacific girls were not achieving as highly in NCEA Level 3 English as their Level 2 English results led us to anticipate. Our anecdotal evidence suggested that achievement levels were affected by a loss of confidence, competing demands from leadership roles and co-curricular activities, and a struggle to maintain motivation in their studies.

Lower achievement averages in national qualifications and standardised testing has prompted the Ministry of Education to label Pacific students "priority learners" (Ministry of Education, 2013). One of the risks of this approach is that defining an educational

> *Carol's study was designed to understand the mismatch between teachers' expectations and the outcomes for students in Year 13 English.*

> *Carol's analysis of the literature identified studies of stereotype threat, the importance of culturally inclusive learning environments, and teacher–student relationships.*

problem by ethnicity can lead to stereotyping, which in turn can lead to decision making that is detrimental to learners: low expectations, less challenging work, limited pathways, and limited access to higher education. Stereotypes can be so pervasive that they directly affect the achievement of minority groups.

Actively valuing the cultural capital of students is recognised as important in fostering more equitable outcomes for students. The potential enablers for Pacific students include the teacher having a knowledge of the learner and a willingness to use this knowledge to make the learning environment culturally inclusive, providing a sense of belonging, validating the learner's own cultural capital, and enabling cultural capital to inform the learning.

My mixed methods approach was informed by Creswell's (2013) transformative model which seeks to "address a social issue for a marginalized or underrepresented population and engage in research that brings about change" (p. 546). This matched my intent: to learn from Pacific students their perceived barriers or enablers to success in Level 3 English, and to gain insight as to how to best meet their needs.

> Carol conducted her study in two phases. In the first phase, she used the schools' NCEA to understand the issue. In the second, she talked with Year 13 girls about their experiences.

NCEA Level 2 and 3 data were collected from the school for the previous 2 years' cohorts. The data were matched; students who were not part of Year 12 and 13 cohorts were excluded. A Grade Point Average (GPA) was calculated for each student for both years and then plotted on a scatter graph to illustrate the difference in achievement between Level 2 and Level 3 for each student. The data were disaggregated; separate graphs were created for Pacific and non-Pacific students to identify whether there were different patterns for the two groups.

> Carol had to go beyond looking at 'averages' of both groups because of the variation apparent when she plotted the data on a scatterplot.

For both cohorts, the highest achieving Level 2 Pacific girls had a lower GPA in Level 3, while their non-Pacific counterparts showed an increase. However, at the same time a good proportion of the Pacific students improved. We described the data for Pacific students as 'volatile'; NCEA Level 2 English data was not as a reliable predictor of their achievement in Level 3 as it was for the majority of non-Pacific students. This finding would suggest the importance of using data that can inform teaching of individual students rather than to determine wholesale pathways for groups of students.

Because the aim of the work was primarily to learn from the Pacific participants, I wanted to use the Pacific research methodology of talanoa (Vaioleti, 2006). The aim of using talanoa was to learn *from* the students not just about them. By taking this approach, I hoped to enable participants to direct the pace and direction of the interviews, privileging the topics they wanted to focus on.

> *Carol chose a research methodology to acknowledge and mitigate the difficulties of having a dual role as teachers and researcher.*

Six Pacific students from the 2014 Level 3 English cohort were interviewed twice over the course of the study—early in Term 2 and then again in Term 3. The first interview began with demographic questions about the students' cultural identity, family, first language, school, and out-of-school commitments and aspirations. Students rated their perceptions of Level 3 English in relation to Level 2 English and their other subjects. The remaining questions were open-ended, encouraging the students to discuss their views of English content and pedagogy.

The cases highlighted the diversity among the six participants despite being a small sample of Pacific students. At the time of the interviews, results for internal assessments completed so far showed that five of the six participants were exceeding their Level 2 English grades. However, the factors that acted as enablers and barriers for success in Level 3 English were different for the individual students, and the enablers and barriers interacted in different ways. Relationships with teachers, while valued, did not tend to dictate the participants' achievement. Similarly, the ability of teachers to help students make a personal connection to the course content did not correspond in a simple way to each students' academic engagement. External factors such as leadership roles, home obligations, and co-curricular and church commitments at times created pressure but at others provided the skills and attributes to succeed

> *Factors that at times worked as barriers at other times worked as enablers for the students.*

in the classroom. This suggests the combinations of enablers and barriers are perhaps more important than the type of enablers and barriers themselves.

Some participants in this study, while still identifying and being identified by their Pacific ethnicities, felt that they were losing a connection with aspects of their cultural identities. Only one participant in this study reported confidence in maintaining her language; all described some tension at home as a result of their heritage language being less commonly used. Tuafuti and McCaffery (2005) stress the importance of "life chances and life choices" for Pacific people (p. 488). They argue the power of culture comes from the individual's right to determine the aspects they maintain and the opportunity to do so. Part of the uncertainty around their identity for four of the participants in this study seemed to stem from a lack of choice and power.

> Carol's findings highlighted the importance of language, of stereotypes, and of motivation.

In addition, the participants in this study were aware of societal stereotypes of Pacific people and the negativity surrounding Pacific students' academic achievement. This had led them to "think less" of themselves and to see themselves as less able than their non-Pacific peers including other ethnic minorities.

All six participants were motivated to succeed at school for their own benefit but also to be a source of pride for their family and to inspire younger siblings. However, in addition to this, the participants saw achieving academic success particularly important as "an Islander". This seemed to suggest that the participants saw themselves as representatives of all Pacific people; as if they had a personal responsibility to contradict stereotypes of their entire multi-ethnic community. This challenge served as a motivator but was also overwhelming for the individual.

The volatility of Pacific students' data in this study raises questions about how data are used and how they inform the decision-making processes in schools about things such as streaming, course allocations, and the breadth of the curriculum to which students are given access. In order to achieve the ambitious goals identified in documents such as the Pasifika Education Plan, a more nuanced approach needs to be taken in prioritising Pacific learners. Priority needs to be given to approaches that further the success of high-achieving Pacific students. Ultimately, the perceived enablers for these Pacific girls in NCEA Level 3 English seemed to be the combination of teaching practices and experiences outside the classroom that supported their learning at a particular time. Classroom-based enablers needed to be combined with other enablers, including those from the students' lives outside of the teaching environment. Some factors that are often framed as barriers for Pacific students, such as having responsibility for younger siblings, were in some cases enablers for the participants in this study. Only the students themselves can provide teachers with insight into the individual's barriers and enablers, and how these factors are interacting. For that reason, a little talanoa with our Pacific students could go a long way to making this happen.

> *Carol concluded that barriers and enablers were different at different times for different students. Assumptions about barriers and enablers, Carol argues, are another type of stereotype threat for Pacific youth.*

Chapter 2 Overcoming a plateau in mathematics learning

Trish Holster

The purpose of this study was to identify possible reasons why a significant number of students at my primary school were not making the expected rate of progress from stage 5 to stage 6 of the numeracy progression (from early to advanced additive thinking). The concern arose from an annual school self-review. Limiting the project to profiling the issue for one point in students' numeracy development (additive thinking) allowed me to look at a range of possible constraints on learning and to identify ways to accelerate student achievement.

> *Trish's school was struggling to understand why students were not progressing as they should in numeracy.*

Longitudinal data showed that large numbers of boys and girls of all ethnic groups experienced an extended time at stage 5, regardless of whether they were early high achievers, average-performing or under-achieving students. Prior to the study, longitudinal data for students 'stuck' at stage 5 did not show any clear pattern of gaps in students' number knowledge. The research was designed to 'cast a wide net' in order to bring the problem itself into sharper focus.

> *A narrow focus allowed Trish to investigate as many factors as she could that had potential impact.*

Mathematics literature suggested many different explanations for under-achievement in numeracy generally, as well as for difficulties specific to additive thinking. These explanations varied in their level of focus (student, teacher/classroom, and school / wider system) as well as in their theories about learning. To deal with the large number of potential frames and explanations, I created three broad clusters of explanations from literature. These were: student knowledge gap explanations (student level); assessment practice explanations (teacher/system level); and opportunity to learn explanations (teacher/system level).

> Trish used the literature to develop a frame to understand possible explanations at three levels:
> • student
> • teaching
> • assessment.

Five sources of data were used to profile patterns of teaching and learning. These included two quantitative sources, comprising existing longitudinal student achievement data and an anonymous teacher questionnaire about assessment practices. Additionally, three qualitative data sources were used: student numeracy interviews; teacher interviews; and existing 'target-setting' documents used by teachers to set and plan for a term's learning target for one or two low-achieving students in each their class.

> Trish used multiple sources of data to understand students' knowledge, their opportunities to learn, and the influence of assessment. Analysing the data as she went along helped her to use one source to understand another.

The pragmatic mixed-methods approach met the needs of a problem-based research project about achievement in one specific school. Data analysis methods were predetermined, but inferences made at each stage of the research influenced what I did at later stages.

Additionally, the iterative process of data sharing with participants allowed emerging findings to be challenged, and further issues and questions to be identified. This process provided an opportunity to connect what appeared to be salient for teachers when making decisions, to actual learning outcomes (patterns of strength and gaps) for students.

> Trish was mindful of methodological constraints when working in small settings where people know each other.

Analysis of longitudinal data to describe the nature of the 'plateau' (extended time at stage 5) set the scene for the study by identifying a 'summer drop' in learning as a key factor. A very particular pattern of gains and losses in learning over summer surfaced. This raised questions relevant to all three explanation types, knowledge gaps, assessment practices, and opportunity to learn.

Exploring assessment practices created opportunity to better understand the 'summer drop', which converged with evidence of some confusion about the boundary between stage 5 and stage 6 (teacher interviews); a 'summative assessment' orientation (teacher survey); a tendency to ignore students' previous achievement levels (target-setting sheets); and evidence that some incorrect levelling was indeed occurring (student interviews, discussed below).

> *Insight came from through convergence of a number of factors identified across the data sources.*

Exploring student knowledge gaps involved analysis of in-depth student numeracy interviews. Typical case sampling was used to choose the four students, with the aid of criteria that described a 'typical' stage 5 student. These interview data raised a question of accuracy in school longitudinal data, as three of the four 'stage 5 students' clearly showed stage 6 thinking. Although generalisations could not be made from the small non-random sample, this finding converged with a combination of summer drop and assessment practice issues mentioned above.

A pattern of knowledge strengths and gaps—that had not been identified by the standardised assessment tools—emerged that resonated with literature. These findings were consistent with later findings about teacher practices in setting student achievement targets, use of teacher strategies, and use of mathematical representations (e.g., Did a representation such as money or Dienes blocks match the student learning need and the lesson purpose?). Again, although individual findings from small non-random samples were not necessarily robust by themselves, the convergence of data from a range of different sources makes the claims much stronger.

> *While each data source could only provide 'non-significant' results, the combined weight of evidence began to support an emerging hypothesis.*

Opportunity to learn was largely explored through analysing pre-existing 'target-setting sheets' to identify the achievement goals, topics, teaching strategies, and representations teachers focused on when accelerating learning for low achievers. These findings were consistent with student interviews. The gaps previously seen in student performance (numeracy interviews) mapped on to gaps in teacher practices visible in target-setting sheets. Although the data could only hint at biases in classroom programmes, a clear pattern across all target sheets was seen, and the pattern (place value knowledge) did resonate very strongly with specific issues raised in literature about effective numeracy teaching.

The detailed picture we developed of teaching and learning numeracy in the school did not lead to adopting a single explanation of the achievement problem. Instead it highlighted how complex the problem of raising achievement was. Specific actions were developed to fine-tune the mathematics curriculum, classroom teaching practices, and our school-wide moderation meetings. Our emphasis on creating opportunities for staff to share effective pedagogical tools with colleagues, and on introducing new ideas, increased.

The small size of the purposive sample meant it was critically important that the focus was on describing rather than on generalising. I was very aware of potential biases that may have influenced results, such as researcher bias, social desirability bias in teacher interviews, and bias resulting from wording and question order in the questionnaire. Thus, high quality of inference is clearly an important criterion for quality research.

The combination of skills and understandings that I gained throughout this research supported more frequent data discussions with team leaders and the mathematics curriculum team particularly. The reciprocal sharing of data analysis/visualisation tools has been significant in supporting conversations about learning and teaching. Over time, with the school principal's guidance, data discussions about mathematics and literacy learning become commonplace throughout the school. Increased teacher confidence in discussing data with colleagues led to a formalised system of teacher–student conferences integrated with studio (multi-classroom) teaching. This in turn supported student-led conferences with parents.

Trish has used her skills as researcher in her role as leader, using evidence about learning and teaching as an artefact to focus professional conversations with staff.

Chapter 3 Does Samoan Bilingual education make a difference?

Jacqui Tutavake

The number of bilingual units within mainstream New Zealand schools is expanding. Inclusion of bilingual units within mainstream schools is important to ensure that there are sufficient opportunities for students to develop and achieve in learning environments that are inclusive of their first language, cultural backgrounds, and experiences (May, Hill, & Tiakiwai, 2006). This study was informed by existing literature that suggests Samoan Bilingual units can have significant positive results for student achievement. There is also considerable research that supports the importance of maintaining culture and language. The Pasifika Education Plan (2008–12) included goals that were "enhancing language proficiency as foundation for learning and achievement, maintenance and preservation" (Ministry of Education, 2007b).

In 2009, a Samoan Bilingual unit was established in a low-decile school in Auckland after the community expressed a need for one, with almost half the school identifying as Samoan. This study profiled the unit 3 years after its establishment, to determine whether

School initiatives are a common source of inquiry, allowing schools to investigate whether things are working as they were intended.

there had been a positive impact on student achievement. Enrolments in the unit had grown from 23 students across Years 1–3 in 2009 to 72 students from Years 0–6 students in 2012.

The design for this study involved using a group of Samoan Bilingual unit students (N=10) with a similar number of Samoan students (N=12) in the mainstream school, and comparing the English reading achievement of students in each group, across the 3-year time period. The *Supplementary Test for Achievement in Reading* (STAR)[1] was used as the reading assessment tool for this research.

> The use of two groups of comparable students provides an indication of the difference effects of the 'treatment' over time.

To supplement the quantitative achievement data, I also collected qualitative data by asking parents and teachers about their perceptions of the benefits of Samoan Bilingual education because we saw this not only as important but essential. The incorporation of more informal interview techniques allowed for consideration of context and participants as interviews were more free-flowing and responsive rather than prescriptive. The methodology termed talanoa (Vaioleti, 2003) is a flexible and interactive approach that "provides a culturally appropriate setting for the researcher and those researched to talk spontaneously about whatever arises" (Fletcher, Parkhill, Fa'afoi, & O'Regan, 2009, p. 26).

> Collecting parent and teacher voices enabled findings to become more nuanced, adding a level of richness and depth to the quantitative findings.

The analyses revealed that students in the bilingual unit achieved accelerated progress in STAR over time, progressing from a mean stanine of 2.4 in February 2010 to a mean stanine of 4.8 by the end of 2012. In contrast, the sample of Samoan students from mainstream classes made expected but not accelerated progress across the 3-year period. A large difference was that students in the bilingual unit made more progress than other students over summer.

> Raw (unprocessed) data often require a level of 'cleaning' to prepare for analysis. This might include checking that students are matched correctly over time, that all scores are within acceptable ranges, and that students' age, gender and ethnicities are correctly entered.

---

1 Published by NZCER, 2011.

Interview data were analysed using thematic analysis. Parents and teachers each identified similar benefits and challenges. The interviews with bilingual unit teachers showed that building relationships with parents and fanau was a priority, followed closely by language enrichment and language maintenance. In addition, teachers commented on the increased creativity of students and teachers within the unit, necessitated by the need to create new words that are not found in Samoan. They also suggested that students in the unit were more engaged and enthusiastic in their learning.

> Stanines are standardised according to year level. If a student is making expected progress, their stanine over time should remain the same. Thus, any increase in average stanine indicates a potential shift.

Parents indicated that the closer home–school connection and language enrichment opportunities were the primary reasons for placing their children in the bilingual unit. Parents also believed that the unit helped to instil cultural identity and pride in their children. These qualitative and quantitative findings together indicate that home–school partnerships, language enrichment, student engagement, and belonging may directly contribute to student achievement.

> Jacqui used the qualitative data to help her understand what might contribute to the outcomes.

This study allowed me to develop research and analysis skills personally, and has contributed to the somewhat limited research literature on the efficacy of Samoan bilingual units. However, looking back now, two changes to the design would have strengthened this research. First, while the opportunity for a translator or speaker of the Samoan language was offered to parents and teachers, none took up the offer. If I were to do this inquiry again I would make it easier for participants to engage in interviews in their first language, as of right.. Secondly, given the context and the focus of this study, in future research I would seek to use bilingual assessments in parallel with the English tests as outcome measures.

> *No study is perfect and no study finds all the answers. As with all studies, there are some aspects that Jacqui would do differently if she were to conduct her study over again.*

Chapter 4 Patterns of literacy progress, achievement, and the development of self-regulating young readers in a high-decile school

Liz Lapish

Within the New Zealand context, National Standards have formalised the expectations for achievement. The present study responded to a context-specific need identified by the collection of National Standards data. In response to a perceived lack of progress by students in a high-decile school, I sought to identify how the teaching and learning of reading could be developed to improve rates of student progress.

> *Liz's school was concerned that students should be making more progress than they were.*

The research literature was used to explore how students might develop a self-extending system for reading. A self-extending system is the 'in-the-head' control which over time leads to empowerment of the student to assume agency to engage in increasingly difficult texts (Clay, 1991). The literature on learning to read was synthesised with the literature on self-regulation. A self-regulating reader is one who is expertly adaptive, monitoring and adjusting strategies and behaviours, while judging and adapting self-performance in relation to reading goals.

The research suggested that the overall goal of reading literacy instruction is to develop flexibility and adaptability in students to draw from and use the whole range of possible strategies interchangeably. Students can develop self-extending systems through engaging in meta-cognitive (thinking about thinking) discussions during instruction. This understanding underpinned the focus of observations and interviews, and provided a lens which supported the analysis of the data.

The literature provided Liz two interacting frames to guide her study: research on learning to read, and research on self-regulation. Liz brought these together to consider how children might develop self-extending systems for reading.

My study comprised two distinct stages. The first was to understand patterns of student reading outcomes. The second was to understand their reading behaviours in class, in response to the instruction they received. Initially the research sought to establish the existing levels of Year 1 and Year 2 student reading achievement. Reading group observations and interviews were used to understand the ways in which students and their teachers developed self-regulatory behaviours and strategies during reading instruction.

Answering the research questions required two sequential phases to first identify and then explain the data. This was an Explanatory Sequential Mixed Methods (ESMM) approach. A profile of reading achievement was developed by drawing from the schools' database of 2014 reading assessment results. The quantitative reading achievement data analysis also supported the development of questions to be asked during the teacher interviews. An overview of how the research design aligns to the ESMM research model is presented in Figure 4.1.

Liz divided her study into phases so she could focus first on patterns of learning outcomes and then learning processes.

Figure 4.1 *Overview of main research question and sub questions*

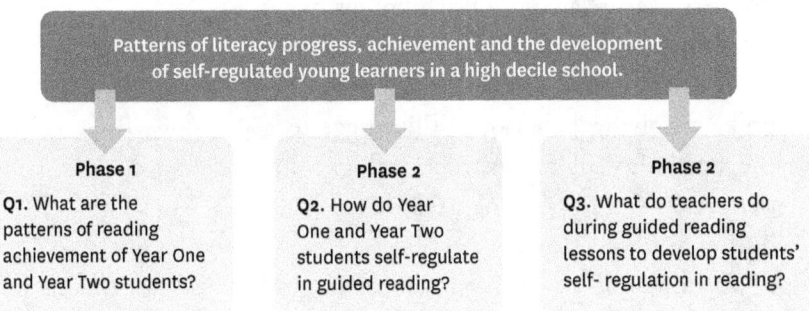

In Phase 1 students' test results were examined, including school entry alphabet knowledge, basic sight word knowledge, and reading level. Individual students' patterns of progress were analysed by tracking students across different testing points. The results were summarised to show patterns across time by presenting data analysis in a series of figures and tables.

In Phase 2 data I collected data through teacher and student interviews alongside guided reading lesson observations. Interviews were coded by thematic responses and analysed using the process of scrutinising, cataloguing, and arranging responses systematically in groups according to salient issues, concepts, and themes which emerged from recurring views and responses from participants in relation to the interview questions. Teachers' and students' interactions and independent behaviours were analysed separately. The frequency of reading strategies used during monitoring and problem solving were identified and categorised, alongside any self-regulatory feedback students received.

Liz's observations of students' use of strategies in their reading groups led her to develop the hypothesis of a gap in students' problem-solving abilities.

Students' strategy use was most often focused on visual cue sources. An initial teacher focus on decoding did not appear to support acceleration for learners, even those who entered school with high levels of alphabet knowledge and word knowledge. Students across all reading colour bands were observed often to seek and rely on teacher support or confirmation during numerous monitoring or problem-solving demands.

The main explanation for the lack of progress was related to teaching for self-regulation. Students were observed to rely on teacher support, rather than engage in problem-solving behaviour. This suggested the possibility of an instructional gap in the patterns of responding used by teachers during reading lessons.

> Liz's observations of students' use of strategies in their reading groups led her to develop the hypothesis of a gap in students' problem-solving abilities.

Examination of teacher practices in guided reading sessions were used to ascertain how teachers developed students' capacity to adaptively self-regulate, and if metacognition was developed.

The overall findings indicated that students' reading behaviours reflected the instructional practices of teachers. Metacognitive discussions were observed sparingly, and were not explicit. The possible explanation for the learning patterns therefore was that instruction was not yet supporting self-regulatory reading. Teachers monitored students' reading success and taught a focus on visual cues, rather than developing students' self-regulatory capability through engaging with them in metacognitive conversations. The hypothesis was that opportunity exists for students to develop skills to monitor their own success and their own flexible use of reading strategies.

The study concluded that gaps in students' strategies could be addressed through specific teaching approaches. Even in contexts where there has been very effective professional learning in the past, changes in teaching staff over time mean that teachers may no longer have the same shared understandings about students' learning processes.

> Liz noticed strong alignment between students' help-seeking, rather than problem-solving, behaviours and teachers' confirmations of students' errors or successes.

In this study, the link between guided reading, metacognitive conversations, reading strategies, and self-regulated reading was not yet a feature of the participating teachers' practice in the teaching of reading.

> Liz argues that specific changes to practice would help build students' capability to monitor their own reading and engage in problem-solving behaviours while they read. However, she argues that it cannot be assumed that teachers know how to implement these changes without support.

PART 2 INQUIRING INTO TEACHING AND OPPORTUNITIES TO LEARN

Aaron Wilson

At first sight, the six studies in this section look to be very different from one another. They cover vastly different levels of schooling, ranging from Caroline's study of vocabulary teaching in Year 1–3 classrooms, to Rochelle's investigation of academic counselling in Year 13. They also cover a wide range of valued student outcomes from a highly specific focus on aspects such as vocabulary learning (Caroline) or a particular English NCEA achievement standard (Richard), to a focus on academic achievement more generally (Sue, Rochelle, and Lynne). Also, while five of the studies were primarily concerned with improving academic achievement outcomes, Kerry's focus was on the key competency of managing self.

Despite these differences, the studies in this section had much in common. Most importantly, all the scholars were focused on developing a better understanding of the complex relationships between current patterns of teaching and current patterns of student learning. The approaches they used to develop an understanding of that very complex relationship shared many common features. There is much in what they did within their own settings to understand specific issues that we think is generalisable to other settings and other issues.

First and foremost, all the scholars adopted an agentic view of teachers and teaching. A key assumption of their studies was that, notwithstanding the influence of factors outside of school such as those related to socio-economic status, changing what teachers did could have a positive impact on valued learning outcomes. They wanted to understand what teachers currently knew and did because they genuinely believed that understanding and then refining that knowledge and those practices could lead to improved outcomes for learners.

A hallmark of the scholars in this section, and throughout this book, was their intellectual curiosity. They had all noticed something that created an itch to find out more. All of the studies had as a starting point anecdotal data or even just a feeling that things were not going quite as well as they might. In some cases, the scholars already had quite strong data to support their hunch that current teaching or interventions were not having the impact that had been hoped for, or at least not in all areas or for all learners. For Rochelle, Sue, and Lynne, their study schools had implemented interventions with promising results but they wanted more detailed information about how teachers had enacted new approaches and/or how students had responded to these approaches, in order that the interventions could be fine-tuned. Kerry's study took place at a very early stage of a digital innovation prompted by teachers' and parents' concerns about students' ability to manage their learning in an environment assumed to provide more potential distractions at the same time as giving more student choice.

The starting points for Caroline and Richard were to do with student achievement data that had highlighted a gap between desired and actual student outcomes. Their analysis of these data had indicated that while there had been improvements overall, there were specific learning outcomes and groups of students where improvements had not been achieved. In Caroline's case, a school-wide focus on reading was associated with improved achievement in some aspects of reading—but not in vocabulary. In Richard's case, students' achievement in NCEA English had improved for all students on average, but non-Pasifika students had improved more than Pasifika students, meaning that an existing gap had actually got wider. The data that prompted their studies shaped the scope of their projects—they were able to design a more tailored study because they had specific ideas about which groups and what content should be the focus of their efforts.

The scholars were all concerned with effective teaching which they defined as teaching that makes a positive difference for valued learning outcomes. Implicit in all the studies, notably in the prominence given to student voice, was the notion that teaching is situated and contingent. We see the view of effective teaching taken by the scholars as consistent with that articulated in the *New Zealand Curriculum* (Ministry of Education, 2007a): "Since any teaching strategy works differently in different contexts for different students, effective pedagogy requires that teachers inquire into the impact of their teaching on their students." (p. 35). None of the scholars applied a checklist approach where they simply looked to see how closely teachers were adhering to a set of teaching practices identified as generically "best practice". However, each of the scholars did look to the research literature to identify teaching practices for which there was strong evidence of effectiveness. Without assuming that importing such practices would achieve desired outcomes for students in their specific context, identifying these evidence-based practices was vital for generating and shaping hypotheses about why current instruction was or was not having the desired effects on student outcomes in their context.

All of the scholars used a mixture of qualitative and quantitative data to develop a rich picture of teaching in their particular contexts. The qualitative and quantitative analyses served different purposes and the studies were all the stronger for including both types of analysis. Take the quantitative data from questionnaires and qualitative analysis of interviews, for example. Caroline, Rochelle, Sue, Lynne, and Kerry all used an anonymous student questionnaire to get a general overview of patterns in students' perceptions or knowledge. Using a questionnaire in this way meant that the scholars could get a general overview of patterns from a relatively large number of participants. The anonymity of the questionnaires was an important consideration here because students were commenting directly or indirectly on their own teachers, and the scholars wanted students to be able to express their opinions as openly and honestly as possible. The quantitative data alone though would have limited what the Lead Teachers could learn from their students. The five scholars who included a survey all followed this up with semi-structured interviews with individual or focus groups of students to get a more detailed and nuanced understanding of their perceptions.

Although, unlike the others, Richard's study was primarily qualitative, he used quantitative NCEA data in the sampling phase of his project to identify English teachers whose Pasifika students had made more than normal progress, before using a range of qualitative measures to try to explain why they might be so effective for their Pasifika learners. The quantitative aspect of his study made it much stronger, as it provided a robust and independent means of identifying teachers most likely to be using practices effective for Pasifika learners. Kerry, too, used analyses of quantitative data early on in her study to identify students with higher and lower levels of self-regulation. Like Richard, Kerry used the quantitative data as the basis of purposive sampling. In her case she aimed to use the differences between the two groups of students to better understand factors that could be leveraged for the development of self-regulation.

It is not always the case that those who design programmes on behalf of students ask those students, as the supposed beneficiaries of changed teaching and learning opportunities, what they think should be changed about teaching and learning in that context, or what their experience has been. But all the scholars in this section placed a very strong emphasis on student voice, whether from questionnaires, interviews, or focus groups. Student voice in these studies served both as a mirror and a window and afforded the scholars new perspectives on teaching and learning. In Caroline's study, student voice was a mirror in that it allowed her to look at a lesson she had observed from another angle—the perspective of students in the classroom. This led her to identify that there was at times a mismatch between the vocabulary learning the teachers had assumed or hoped would have occurred, and the actual learning the students had achieved. In the same study, student voice also served as a window, allowing Caroline to gain insight into aspects of the child's knowledge and experiences previously unknown, and otherwise unknowable, to her. Specifically, Caroline asked students to share a lexicon of words related to something they enjoyed doing outside of schools. Without asking students this, she would not have had a window into this important aspect of their language experience.

Another key theme across the studies was how differences within the data (variability) were used as a key way of identifying what worked well and what did not. In Caroline's case, the variability was related not to different teachers or groups of children but to different aspects of reading. She came to the study wondering why teaching approaches seemed to be more effective for some aspects of reading, such as sentence comprehension, than they appeared to be for vocabulary development. The variability in different aspects of reading enabled her to gather additional data about the specific aspect where gains were less than desired. Richard used variability in student outcomes to identify teachers whose students over 2 successive years had achieved particularly positive results in the NCEA standard. Lynne, similarly, identified tutor classes where students, on average, had much higher and much lower knowledge about the requirements of NCEA than others. This helped her identify one avenue of inquiry as to why the academic counselling programme at the school was differentially effective. Being able to find similarities and differences in the responses of different groups to teaching and learning opportunities is a powerful way of finding out more about what works for whom and under what circumstances.

Finally, while all six had an explicit focus on fine-tuning teacher practice so that more desirable outcomes could be achieved, none of them was in a rush to implement changes. All were highly committed to taking their time, being methodical, and developing a very rich and detailed profiling of current patterns of teaching and learning before recommending new approaches or refinements. Doing this requires rigour and restraint. They all resisted the urge to solve problems until they fully understood those problems. Although none of their studies were strictly speaking intervention studies, what they each found out provided a very clear direction for future intervention. All the scholars identified strengths in current teacher practice or knowledge that could be built on as well as gaps, misunderstandings, and areas for development. They finished their scholarship with questions as well as answers. They all had clear ideas for transforming teaching and learning within their schools, but they also had identified areas where they now wanted more information. Fortunately, they all felt confident that they had developed inquiry skills they could use to answer those questions.

Chapter 5 Patterns of vocabulary instruction in Years 1–3 following professional development

Caroline Chawke

This study took place in a decile 2 primary school in South Auckland. Achievement data across the school had shown annual accelerated progress in standardised reading tests, specifically in word recognition, sentence comprehension, and paragraph comprehension. However, vocabulary scores were not rising at the same accelerated rate, and there was a concern that a relative lack in vocabulary would negatively impact comprehension levels in succeeding years. Years 1–3 were chosen as a focus to maximise the school's future potential to accelerate progress in vocabulary based on findings from the study.

A literature review identified a gap in research relating to effective vocabulary teaching and learning, and in particular, a gap in triangulated data which examines the interactions of practice, beliefs, and knowledge. This project sought to illustrate the ways in which teacher practices, teachers' beliefs and understandings, and students' use of targeted vocabulary, might impact achievement in standardised tests.

Despite continued improvement in reading, students' vocabulary levels had not improved. This discrepancy motivated closer inquiry.

To conduct this research I used a mixed methods, case-study approach. Qualitative data were transcribed and analysed to elicit key themes. These themes were then quantified to determine their relative frequency. Quantitative data were recorded and counted. The themes and counts were then triangulated to provide a cohesive picture of the teaching and learning of vocabulary teaching within the classrooms.

Four teachers of Years 1–3 classes agreed to take part in the study. For these teachers, the research involved three measures. First, the researcher conducted an evaluation of the classroom environment to collect evidence about the number of language-rich features present in classrooms. This evaluation used a 10-point binary (yes/no) evaluation framework and included items on display, published student materials, and seating layout. Secondly, each teacher was observed once during an ordinary reading lesson. These lessons each had two parts; one was an emphasis on vocabulary during shared reading, the second was instructions around follow-up vocabulary tasks. Finally, each teacher was interviewed by the researcher to ascertain perceptions around the goal of the lesson, the deliberate acts of teaching involved, the choice of text(s) used, and their own perceptions about the efficacy of the lesson.

> Through recruiting teachers as volunteers, Caroline took an in-depth look into four teachers' practice as case studies, allowing her to gather rich understanding of these examples.

In addition, 12 students agreed to be interviewed, with their parents' consent. These students were each interviewed within 1 hour of the lesson that had been observed, to maximise students' recall of the lesson. Students were asked to recall the focus vocabulary they had been taught during the lesson, and their recollections about the strategies that teachers used to help them learn that vocabulary. They were also asked about vocabulary on topics that they found interesting (interest words) as well as academic vocabulary from the lesson (academic words).

The triangulated findings indicated three key themes. Classrooms tended to be vocabulary-rich learning environments; across the four classrooms, 88% of the criteria of the classroom environment evaluation were present, indicating that teachers had set up stimulating environments for their learners. Another finding was that teachers used two different approaches to teaching vocabulary. The first was a focus on word definition of key words. The second included extended instruction around targeted academic vocabulary. In general, teachers tended to use the first approach more often than the second, and instruction tended to be focused on Tier 1 vocabulary (basic words, such as 'book', 'girl', 'sad', 'run'). I hypothesised that this was because these are words that teachers believe are important to focus on, and evidence for this was provided in the teacher interviews. For example, Teacher A explained the words she thought were important for students to learn:

> Caroline's evidence suggested that teachers believed they should focus on basic words because children did not know them, and students did struggle to remember taught words in lessons. However, from her interviews with children, Caroline discovered that the children did learn large numbers of high-interest words.

> *The essential words, writing as well as reading words are important. And once they have got the basics then I think we can add more technical vocabulary, which goes with certain contexts. Because if they don't have the essential words it won't fall into place together.* (Teacher A)

However this finding was not universal; one teacher who had a higher focus on Tier 2 (high frequency/multiple meaning) words said this:

> *Well they need to obviously know the academic language but being really specific in different areas, so knowing their maths language, knowing their science language, knowing their different curriculum areas academic language. Knowing their concept language.* (Teacher C)

Finally, and perhaps unsurprisingly, student interviews indicated that students struggled to articulate the newly taught focus words from the lesson—about half did not articulate any focus words learned, and about half articulated one taught word from the lesson. When asked about strategies that students recalled their teachers using to help them learn new words, all students indicated the 'sound it out' strategy. This strategy was mentioned three times more often than others, such as writing out the word, or using pictures to help decode the word. Students were also asked about the words associated with topics that students found interesting, in order to provide a broader assessment of their productive vocabulary. The interviews indicated that students knew about three times' more 'interest' vocabulary than 'academic' vocabulary. Additionally, their understanding of interest words was far higher; about 70% of 'interest' words were given a basic or explicit definition by the students, compared with about 10% of academic words.

These combined findings lead to two questions for further investigation at the school level:

1. As students were capable of learning and using a range of 'interest' words, we should consider whether the current vocabulary tests are an accurate measure of their level of vocabulary.
2. What ways can students, teachers, and the learning environment work together to create the same motivation and strategies for learning academic words?

Nationally, it would be of interest to see whether these patterns are consistent across Years 1–3 classrooms. Also, it would be of interest to see whether there is a tendency for New Zealand teachers to focus on Tier 1 words in the classroom, and to consider if this an appropriate focus to enhance student learning of vocabulary.

> *Caroline argues that students were capable of learning and using a high range of interest words, and that these skills should be acknowledged in assessments. Moreover, these skills can be the basis of school strategies to build vocabulary.*

Chapter 6 Effective academic counselling for Māori students in a Northland high school

Rochelle Telfer

In 2010, our school (a co-educational decile 2 school in Northland with 80% Māori students) implemented an academic counselling initiative to help raise student achievement. Academic counselling involves teachers (in our case, whānau/form teachers) meeting with students to establish goals and co-construct plans and pathways to meet these goals. The school believed the changes were positive but we wanted to evaluate students' perspectives of its effectiveness.

> *Rochelle's study arose from a need to evaluate a programme in her school from the point of view of the students.*

The research question was developed by identifying key aspects of effective academic counselling and investigating how our academic counselling measured up in those areas. To maintain a tight focus, the research only considered the Personal Learning Plan (PLP), an interview between the whānau teacher and the student to set goals and consider progress. These conversations generally take place during the 20 minutes of whānau time, and tend to include conversations about attendance, achievement, engagement, and students' goals. Only Year 13 students were involved in the research as Year 13 is a high-stakes year and university entrance is a more complicated qualification than NCEA.

Following the Literature Review, four factors emerged as key aspects of effective academic counselling. First, it appeared that effective academic counselling requires students and teachers to have positive relationships. The large body of research generated by the Te Kotahitanga project (2004–2008) suggests positive relationships between students and teachers would be a key aspect of any successful initiative for Māori students. Secondly, students must be confident in the knowledge of their whānau teachers; and thirdly, the academic counselling must provide effective feedback. This feedback should answer three questions to be effective: Where am I going? How am I going? Where to next? (Hattie & Timperley, 2007). Additionally, the conversations should be driven by students' goals. Conversations about goals should be specific and unambiguous, and achievable and measurable, and should have a commitment from all parties to ensure success (Latham & Locke, 2006).

> The literature provided Rochelle with an evaluation framework with four dimensions:
> - *relational strength*
> - *faith in expertise*
> - *effectiveness of feedback,*
> - *goal directedness.*

As the majority of students at the school were Māori, I decided to use a kaupapa Māori approach when dealing with participants and communicating with those involved. As such, students' perspectives were an integral part of the research. The kaupapa Māori approach to research required a significant shift in my thinking. Two key aspects particularly influenced the approach. First, the research had to be seen to benefit all of the participants; knowledge flows in both directions and the learning is reciprocal (ako). Secondly, the role of the researcher is to join the Māori community in genuine collaboration; research in a Māori context is not possible without "aroha between the participants evidenced by an overriding feeling of tolerance, hospitality, and respect for others, their ideas and opinions" (Bishop, 1998, p. 204).

To determine students' perceptions about the effectiveness of academic counselling within the context of this school, I decided to use two qualitative measures. First, surveys ($n=27$) were used to develop understandings about students' perceptions about the four primary components of effective academic conversations: relationships, knowledge of whānau teacher, feedback, and goals. Secondly, a smaller sample of students (*n*=8) were interviewed to gain more in-depth information. The selection of students for interview used purposive sampling to represent the population of the Year 13 cohort. Thus, it contained five male students and three female students, six of whom identified as Māori and two of whom identified as Pākehā.

> *Rochelle employed principles underlying kaupapa Māori research: benefit for participants through 'ako', and joining the community in genuine collaboration.*

There appeared to be a range of closeness described in the relationships between students and whānau teachers, and some students believed a positive relationship had to be in place prior to the whānau teacher/student relationship. As one student put it, "I don't think you can be expected to sit down with someone and develop a relationship around telling them everything about yourself." However, students who found the PLP useful overall were more likely to feel the PLP helped to improve their relationship with their whānau teacher. The development of positive relationships seemed to be a negotiated process that was driven by students. Understanding of cultural identity was important, particularly for Māori students, but high expectations had the largest impact on students' perceptions of the effectiveness of the academic counselling. In general, students described positive relationships with whānau teachers, and students believed more positive relationships with teachers were associated with higher achievement, for example:

> *She's on my back, but in a good way. Making sure I've got the credits, asking what assessments I'm doing.* (Student A)

> *He cares about everyone. He makes sure that everyone is doing well. And then, in return, we don't muck him over.* (Student B)

There was evidence that student confidence in their whānau teacher's knowledge was an important factor for effective academic counselling, and students generally reported high confidence in the knowledge of their whānau teachers regarding NCEA, as exemplified by this student's statement:

> *With my whānau teacher, she's got a wealth of knowledge especially around exams and knowing the ins and outs of university entrance, numeracy and literacy requirements. Cross-credits—she explains about all that.* (Student C)

However, their perceptions did not always align with the conversations they reported. For example, many students believed their whānau teachers understood university entrance but few reported discussing approved subjects, a key aspect of the university entrance qualification.

Students were generally confident in the feedback provided by whānau teachers. One interesting finding was that while the majority of students believed their teachers had a clear understanding of their current progress and academic trajectory, a large proportion (40%) did not believe the PLP gave *them* a better understanding about their own progress.

The goals the students reported suggested that goal setting was an area that could be improved. It seemed the PLP interview was more helpful for understanding progress ('How am I going?') for students that needed more direction and support in this area, and these tended to be students who were not aiming to gain endorsed certificates. Few students were able to display evidence of effective goal setting strategies when asked to describe the plans in place to meet their goals. Only one student, Student A, was able to describe a specific, measurable plan reporting her intention to "study for 2 hours every night from week seven." The majority of students had vague goals such as "study hard" and "do my work" and there was a predominance of goals associated with learning conditions rather than learning.

> *Rochelle found that while students were generally satisfied with the conversations, there were a number of ways the conversations might be improved to be more useful for students.*

The implementation of effective academic counselling programmes could be a means of addressing some of the disparity in achievement between various groups within New Zealand schools. The development of positive student-teacher relationships is a complicated negotiated process but must be based on a

> *Rochelle concluded that positive relationships needed to have a clear goal—academic success for the student—and that this should be planned for within schools.*

clear goal of teachers to support achievement, particularly for Māori students. This is especially important for students who are new to a school and careful consideration should be given to creating structures within schools that support the development of positive relationships.

This study showed that harnessing student voice can lead to greater understanding of the impact of education initiatives on students. We must find ways to engage regularly with students to learn from these insights and to allow students to feel their voice is heard within their school.

While efforts were made to narrow the focus, on reflection, it was still too large. This is partly due to the large amount of learning for me associated with the implementation of a kaupapa Māori focus.

> *Rochelle concludes that students' perspectives are key to finding out about the impact of initiatives for students' success.*

Chapter 7 Facets of the gemstone: Effective teaching for Pasifika students in Level 2 English

Richard Watkinson

In New Zealand, there is an achievement gap between Pasifika and Palagi (non-Pacific) students. My school had a similar pattern, but the picture was worse for Pasifika students. Achievement rates for NCEA Level 2 were increasing for both groups but the Palagi students figures were improving at a higher rate. The net result was that the achievement gap was growing at my school.

Richard's study emerged from a desire to understand what works for students at risk of not achieving in their school.

I wanted to develop a profile of effective teaching for Pasifika students that followed the model provided by Bishop and Berryman (2006) for Māori students. I was prompted by the despairing request of a colleague who wanted to know "what can I do with my Pasifika students?" My colleague had a deficit mindset and I hoped to be able to change that mindset by providing her with a repertoire of teaching strategies that would improve the achievement of the Pasifika students in her English classes. The Best

Richard wanted to challenge any negative stereotyping of Pasifika students by refocusing the teaching learning relationship.

Chapter 7 Facets of the gemstone: Effective teaching for Pasifika students in Level 2 English

Evidence Synthesis on Teacher Professional Learning and Development (BES) (Timperley, Wilson, Barrar & Fung, 2007) suggests that as teachers learn to use a range of more effective teaching practices their students learn more quickly, the teachers feel more agentic, and the teaching-learning relationship improves. The BES also suggests that, if discourse characterises certain groups as unable to learn, then the discourses need to be challenged. I theorised that understanding effective teaching would challenge some teachers' deficit thinking about Pasifika students.

My review of literature looked at effective teaching practices across subject areas and age groups; in English, and reading in English in particular; and for diverse learners both internationally and in New Zealand. There was a gap in the literature on the subject of effective teaching of English to upper-secondary aged Pasifika students in New Zealand. My study sought to fill this gap.

The body of research on effective teaching is huge. The challenge was to synthesise the information, to pick out the patterns and common ground and the important points of difference between writers. I hypothesised that effective teaching would feature: positive personal and learning relationships between teachers and their Pasifika students; high expectations for student achievement; the use of Pasifika resources; deliberate use of comprehension and literacy strategies; structured group work; apprenticing students into literary habits of mind. I set out to see which, if any, of these approaches were being used by the teachers in the study.

> Richard chose to use a purposive sample by identifying teachers with previous success teaching Pasifika students at Level 2.

Using NCEA pass rates, I identified three effective teachers of Pasifika students in the English departments of two large, mid-decile, state high schools in central Auckland. Using a semi-structured interview structure, I asked each teacher about the elements of their practice they thought contributed to the success of the Pasifika students in their classes. The teacher interviews were analysed to group the data into common themes. This analysis and development of themes helped inform the questions in the student focus groups that followed.

A total of 18 Pasifika students from the two schools took part in focus groups. The students were asked general questions about what teacher actions they thought had helped with their learning in the past; questions about what their current English teacher in particular had done that helped with their learning in English; and about the strategies their current teacher believed would promote achievement. The focus group data was analysed using NVivo to add to and develop new themes about effective teaching. Finally, each teacher was observed teaching her current Level 2 class. Once more, the focus for the observations was informed by the themes developed from the interviews and focus groups.

> Richard used focus groups to gather students' perspectives on what helped their learning.

My research design was influenced by the work of Russell Bishop and Mere Berryman and the Te Kotahitanga project to promote Māori achievement in schools. Bishop and Berryman began their work by interviewing a wide range of young Māori, their whānau, teachers, and principals about their educational experiences. Jan Hill and Kay Hawk (2000) also used "student voice" to determine the importance of teacher–student relationships for Māori and Pasifika students. My decision to use semi-structured focus groups to gather student voice about "what works" for Pasifika students in their NCEA English classes was influenced by the Pasifika concept of talanoa. Vaioleti (2006) characterises talanoa as "respectful, reciprocating interaction. Talanoa is a good conversation, one listens to the other" (p. 26). Because the student focus groups followed the teacher interviews, I asked the students whether the strategies mentioned by their teachers as effective had in fact helped with their learning. In this way the design shared elements of Nakhid's (2003) use of "mediated dialogue" where the researcher presents the ideas from one group of participants in the study to the other.

I hypothesised that positive teacher–student relationships would be a necessary precursor for the success of the strategies. In the interviews, the teachers focused on the strategies they used and rarely talked explicitly about teacher–student relationships. In the focus groups, it was hard to stop the students talking relationships! But as I probed the students' responses it became clear that

> Richard's study was able to 'stand on the shoulders' of previous scholars. A similar design meant that his findings could be compared with previous research, and add nuances based on his own context.

it was the teachers' use of particular strategies that helped to develop positive relationships.

The use of structured, collaborative group work was a crucial element in the process of developing positive relationships. Group work gave Pasifika students the chance to ask each other and their teacher important questions away from the spotlight of whole-class discussions. In whole-class discussions, Pasifika students felt self-conscious about their knowledge and skills, and so they didn't ask or answer questions. In smaller groups they gained confidence from discussions with each other and their teacher and this led to more participation in whole-class discussions. This pattern of student self-efficacy was supported by the lesson observations. There was much more participation by Pasifika students in whole-class discussion in the class where the teacher regularly used structured group work than in the class where the teacher used that strategy rarely.

> *Because Richard had hypotheses driving his investigation, he needed to be careful to look for any evidence that his hypotheses were wrong.*

All the teachers demonstrated that they had high expectations by showing their students examples of merit and excellence level work (the implication was that some teachers showed Pasifika students only 'achieved' level work) and how to achieve that standard. They also gave personalised and positive feedback on student work that included clear guidance on what was needed to achieve at merit and excellence level. The feedback was constructive but also recognised the current levels of effort and achievement. The students appreciated a range of stimulating activities and resources to help deepen their understanding of the written texts.

> *Richard's qualitative investigation allowed him to look at the interactions between the factors of effective teaching.*

Teachers in the study had high levels of subject and pedagogical content knowledge. They also used a range of strategies to teach reading comprehension and went some way towards apprenticing students into literary habits of mind. Interestingly, the teachers did not use Pasifika texts in their classes nor draw upon other Pasifika resources; nor was there evidence of drawing on Pasifika students' cultural strengths or funds of knowledge. This is an area that might be fruitfully explored in the future.

Using group work, providing effective feedback, demonstrating high expectations, and teaching for deeper understanding using appropriate reading strategies and resources all show Pasifika students that their teacher cares about them and about their academic success. Teachers show they care by the practices and strategies they use in their classes and by knowing their students as learners. Teaching strategies and dispositions are interconnected. None are indispensable, one on its own is not sufficient.

> **Richard concludes:** *The title of my thesis used John Hattie's phrase "facets of the gemstone" to characterise effective teaching: "there is no one necessary facet, nor the equal presence of all, but the overlapping of many facets into the whole."*

Chapter 8 Students speak about 'Student Speak': Student perceptions of formative e-assessment results

Susan Smith

The issue investigated arose from teachers' concerns about students' ability to cope with their Student Speak Individual Learning Pathway (SSILP) e-asTTle reports as part of formative assessment at the school. Typically, after a common reading assessment, students' SSILP reports were printed off by the teacher and then shared with the students, in groups, during a reading lesson. It was common practice for students to share and discuss their results with each other and for the teacher to facilitate discussion around the findings. While this might seem like good formative assessment practice, teachers expressed concern that there might be a negative impact on the learning dispositions of these Year 5 students. The purpose of this research was to listen to and better understand what the students themselves thought about the practice, what they learned and how it impacted their approach to learning.

The investigation arose from concerns that Sue and her colleagues shared about possible negative impacts of formative assessment practice on students' relationships and self-belief.

Proponents of formative assessment argue that students should become actively involved participants, collaborating with teachers in non-traditional relationships to form a shared understanding of their current status and 'where to next'. Ideally, they take greater ownership of their learning and benefit most when they are able to evaluate feedback from external sources (Butler & Winne, 1995). It is considered that effective feedback that both informs students, and can be used to improve their performance, can be intrinsically motivating and provide strategically useful information that supports self-regulation (Bangert-Drowns, Kulik, Kulik, & Morgan, 1991).

> Sue's search of the literature identified both positive and negative impacts of formative assessment practices.

But the evidence for formative assessment is not entirely unproblematic. Problems identified include an emphasis on competition over improvement, the assumption that students can readily decode feedback and translate it into action, and a lack of acknowledgement of motivation and belief and the resulting, potentially negative, impact (especially on low-achieving students) (Black & Wiliam, 1998).

> Sue divided her study into phases so that she could get the perspectives of different subgroups of students over time.

The research questions were designed to focus the inquiry to the specific areas of concern: students' self-efficacy, their ability to read the report and make meaning from it, and the impact of having others in the group know your test results, and knowing theirs.

I used a three-stage research process. First, all students completed a brief two-part questionnaire indicating their emotional reactions to their report and their response to it in terms of understanding and use. Secondly, based on the positivity of their scores in each part of the questionnaire, two groups of five students were invited to face-to-face interviews to elaborate on or explain their answers in the questionnaire. In the final stage, an interview question regarding how the students had gone on to use the SSILP reports to establish next learning steps, became the first question of the face-to-face interviews for the second round of data collection (Term 3). Here, they were asked to recall ways in which they had used the reports and the ease/difficulties associated with the process.

> Sue's findings identified a mismatch between teachers' intentions and students' interpretations.

The results showed that students had generally positive emotional reactions to receiving their SSILP reports but a few found the experience unpleasant. Many students explained either their anxiety or their positivity as being linked to their scores. Eighty-five percent of students reported that they looked first at the scores on the report. A common difficulty was the ability to interpret the curriculum level and strand information, and for some students this led to a drop in positivity in Term 3. The proportion of students believing the learning-related feedback was the most important information dropped from Term 2 to Term 3. In Term 3, very few students were able to articulate how their reports had been used for their learning since having received them in Term 2.

Whereas the teachers' intention had been for students to use the curriculum-specific feedback in order to identify next learning steps, students' perceptions of this part of the process were more keenly related to the sharing, and comparing, of scores. Evident from the interview comments of students who felt anxious before receiving their reports, was that their anxiety was related to the scores that were present on the report, rather than any curriculum-specific feedback they might have been expecting.

The findings suggested a cycle, where students with the ability and desire to engage with the feedback subsequently make better use of it for learning and, as a result, are more able and motivated to engage with it next time. Students less able or desirous to engage with the feedback, make less use of it, and perceive it as having little use or relevance, are subsequently less motivated to engage with it next time.

In conclusion then, it was anticipated that use of the SSILP e-asTTle report might unlock the potential learning value of formative assessment. Instead, it would seem that the written report constitutes a potent invitation, but does not guarantee that teaching intentions are understood by all. This study suggests that the key to the use of the report is the preparation and equipping of students to participate in its possibilities.

> *Sue argues that in order for feedback to be formative, 'intersubjectivity' between teacher and students needs to be achieved.*

Chapter 9 Barriers and enablers to students' self-management in BYOD environments

Kerry Boyde-Preece

Increasingly, schools are adopting technologies to provide a platform for the enablement of individualised learning and to raise student engagement. Having a desire to keep abreast of this digital movement, a rural secondary school in Northland embarked on an initiative in 2012 to encourage their students to bring a digital device of their own choosing to support their learning. After 2 years, the school noted that there had been very little uptake by both teachers and students, so in 2015 the school decided to trial a Year 10 Bring Your Own Device (BYOD) pilot class. Parents and teachers had their concerns, many of which surrounded students' ability to manage themselves in digital environments in class. Furthermore, yet to be understood was how self-management might be fostered to promote autonomous self-directed learning. The purpose of the research was to investigate the barriers and enablers to students' self-management in a digital classroom.

> Kerry's study was motivated by a desire to understand what the enablers and barriers were to students' self-management in a BYOD class.

Self-management is one of the five key competencies of the *New Zealand Curriculum* (Ministry of Education, 2007a); however in 2015, when this research was undertaken, there were no national measures in place to evaluate students' self-management. Moreover, the assessment of self-management had been referred to as too difficult partly because it was thought to be woven throughout the curriculum, and partly due to the subjectivity involved (Hamilton, Farruggia, Peterson, & Carne, 2013).

The key competency of self-management is unique to the New Zealand curriculum; however, its foundation lies in international literature based on the theory of self-regulation (Hipkins, 2006). To equate this study within an international context, the philosophy of self-regulation provided the framework and guidelines for the line of inquiry. What motivated the study was understanding how students might move from a reliance on their teachers' direction to being an autonomous independent learner aided by the effective use of digital technologies.

> *Kerry drew from international literature on self-regulation to help her understand the New Zealand-specific term 'self-management'.*

The study was designed to first profile students' self-regulation in the BYOD class utilising an anonymised student survey. This approach produced a snapshot and from this vantage point students could be invited to an interview. This resulted in a small representative group who displayed a mix of self-regulation/self-management. Teachers' opinions were also sought through individual interviews, and parents' opinions were explored through surveys that were coded anonymously to match their child's interview.

> *Kerry's study used both quantitative and qualitative data to understand the issue. A survey allowed her to understand the current general situation. Interviews of a subset allowed her to understand specific contextual factors.*

Crucial to the design was the need to learn what factors were aiding or hindering students' self-regulation when using their own digital device. The student survey allowed students to be grouped into low, moderate, and high self-regulating students. From this vantage point students represented a mix of self-regulating abilities.

The study highlighted three dominant themes that contribute to students' self-management in a BYOD class: the importance of task relevance to students to enable intrinsic motivation, the need to develop parent–teacher relationships to support students' self-management, and the need for ongoing professional development for teachers that specifically focuses on digital integration and student-centred learning.

Kerry interviewed a purposive sample of students based on their level of self-regulation indicated by their survey responses.

Factors that could enable students' self-management in BYOD classes include:

1. a shared language that extends students' interpretation of self-management
2. teachers and their schools investigating what drives the motivation of students in executing self-management strategies
3. effective use of pedagogies in order to enhance learning strategies within a BYOD environment, and
4. parent–school partnerships to support students' self-management.

Participation rates from both students and their parents were relatively low. In this study a parent survey and an invitation to participate were sent out separately. One way of addressing this issue could be to send out any parent survey at the time of inviting parents to participate—in this way parents can see exactly what is involved in the study/survey and may be more inclined to participate. In hindsight, interviewing parents, as well as teachers and students, would have provided a more comprehensive understanding of parents' perspectives and permitted an opportunity to explore communications between parents and teachers.

Kerry concluded that barriers and enablers to self-management were multi-factorial.

She offers four key recommendations for promotion of self-management in the BYOD environment (1) shared language (2) inquiry into students' motivations (3) effective BYOD pedagogy (4) parent/school partnerships.

Chapter 10 Implementation of Academic Counselling by tutor teachers at a low-decile secondary school

Lynne Savage

This project focused on student and teacher knowledge, beliefs, and perceptions about the National Certificate of Educational Achievement (NCEA) and Academic Counselling (AC) in a low-decile urban secondary school.

Lynne's project arose from an innovation in her school, and the need to evaluate whether it was having the intended effects.

The school began AC to improve senior student achievement. The key features of AC at the school were regular scheduled two-way conversations between a student and a designated teacher (Academic Counselling / coaching / mentoring), and periodic three-way parent–student–teacher conversations. The assumption was that academic conversations with students and whānau would be most effective when they were based on quality data about each student's academic progress within the year. It was also vital that they were individualised and the discussion was focused on learning and achievement rather than behaviour.

Student achievement tracking was initially the responsibility of the school's academic dean. Then the pastoral deans took some of the load so more students could have personalised achievement-focussed discussions. Responsibilities were then further shared with tutor teachers (form/homeroom or whānau teachers) of senior classes. Staff-wide professional learning and development (PLD) had been put in place that focused on upskilling tutor teachers so they could take ownership of mentoring their own students.

At the time the study was conducted AC was relatively new at the school and the style of implementation was changing. Although anecdotal evidence had suggested that AC had been effective when led by a dean, it was unclear whether the AC would still be effective when responsibility was shifted more to tutor teachers. Discussions with Senior Leadership Team members with responsibilities for AC supported the idea of collecting baseline data of students' and teachers' knowledge of NCEA and AC. Analysing these data would help the school see how the programme was going and to identify specific ways it could be improved. The hypothesis that underpinned this study was that teachers required developed knowledge of both NCEA and AC for effective implementation of AC in their tutor class. Year 12 was selected as the focus as students would be in the second of their NCEA years and were therefore expected to have some knowledge of the school's processes of AC and requirements for NCEA qualifications.

> Based on her hypothesis, developed from the literature, Lynne sought data about whether teachers and students understood both NCEA and Academic Counselling.

The study used a mixed methods approach. In the first phase Lynne collected data about teachers' and students' knowledge and perceptions of NCEA and AC using a confidential questionnaire. The second and third phases involved observations of a subset of teachers and students during their AC conferences followed by individual semi-structured interviews about their perceptions of their conference. Questionnaires were completed by 56% of the

> Lynne used parallel questionnaires to investigate teachers' and students' knowledge. She also conducted debrief interviews after academic counselling sessions.

Year 12 students (98/179) and 66% of tutor teachers (6/9). Interviews were conducted with four students and two teachers.

The collection and analysis of data about both teacher and student understandings and perceptions were critical for answering the research questions. Triangulation of results was completed with the assumption that the teachers with the most complete and detailed knowledge of NCEA and AC would have conveyed that information to their students who would in turn also demonstrate a better understanding of NCEA and AC. It was hoped therefore that aligning these two key sources of data would improve the reliability of the results.

> *Lynne found that participants were generally positive about the benefits of AC, but that students had low levels of understanding about NCEA, and teachers' knowledge was variable.*

An overarching finding was that AC was generally supported and appreciated by both students and teachers, but there were key areas for development with specific gaps in students' and teachers' knowledge of NCEA and AC. Students and teachers had varied beliefs about who should lead the AC and how it should be implemented. Some felt it better led by a dean whereas others saw benefits for students when the tutor teacher did this.

The teacher questionnaire showed that 83% of teachers were optimistic about the potential of AC but wanted further support in the form of professional learning and development opportunities to implement it more effectively.

Teachers' and students' knowledge of NCEA and AC were each scored out of 12. Students overall demonstrated poor knowledge of NCEA and the AC programme; the median score across all students was only 2. However, analysing students' scores by tutor class showed significant variability with one class having a median student score of 5 and another having a median score of just 1.

Teachers had a very good understanding of NCEA Level 1 requirements, but their understanding of requirements at Levels 2 and University Entrance (UE) were much more varied, with some teachers demonstrating very low knowledge of these requirements. There was also variation in teachers' knowledge of school AC goals. Variations in their knowledge of both NCEA and AC meant tutor teachers implemented AC in their tutor class in different ways.

A major implication for the school from this study was that teachers required more targeted professional development about AC and NCEA. Specifically, it had largely been assumed that teachers were already very familiar with the NCEA requirements for each qualification and for UE, but this was not the case. Because teachers can only give students' quality advice about their academic targets when they have a deep knowledge of the targets the students are aiming for, developing teachers' knowledge of NCEA was a pressing need.

Despite issues in the transfer of responsibility for AC from deans to tutor teachers, there remained significant benefits in having tutor teachers lead this. A distributed leadership model of AC gave tutor teachers the responsibility of providing AC to the students in their class. Time allocated for AC during tutor time gave teachers time to talk with individual students as well as the entire class explicitly about requirements for achievement of each NCEA qualification. Improving teachers' knowledge of NCEA and AC in a scaffolded way will offer tools they can also use in their classrooms. Ongoing professional development and reflection will support teachers to participate in school decision making (Marks & Louis, 1999) which improves the school's capacity for organisational learning. Decisions will be made based on real student voice which means decisions are more likely to have staff buy-in.

As well as learning much useful information about students' and teachers' knowledge of NCEA and AC, Lynne also learnt much about conducting research. In future iterations, she would pilot test the questions to make sure they are written in student-friendly language and include more prompts within the qualitative questions which may help students write more detailed answers. I would also consider including Year 13 students to test the hypothesis that they would have broader knowledge as they have more experience with NCEA.

Lynne's reflections highlighted the importance of 'pilot testing' any tools that are developed for inquiry. Like the other inquiries, this one also sparked further questions for investigation.

PART 3 INQUIRING INTO TEACHERS' PROFESSIONAL LEARNING

Mei Lai

The four chapters in this section inquire into teachers' professional learning. But in each, the lens of the inquiry is focused on different phenomena: (1) the features of the group setting when teachers learn together; (2) the transfer of that learning into practice; (3) the internal sense making that teachers need to do when they are involved in learning communities; and (4) how teams of teachers function well for the benefit of students' learning.

Two of the four studies in this section focus on the processes of Professional Learning Communities within schools, an important global trend in teacher professional learning. Around the world, teachers are increasingly encouraged to collaborate to improve their teaching practices. The assumption is that by working together, teachers will reflect on their own practices, and gain new knowledge and skills through discussion with others in the group. The discussion and collaboration is also intended to support teachers to feel motivated and empowered. This in turn will help them to collaboratively develop more effective teaching practices which will lead to improved student achievement. Such communities have been called by a variety of names, such as communities of practice, professional learning communities, and professional learning networks (e.g., Stoll & Seashore Louis,

2007; Wenger, 1998). In this section, Catherine and Gina use the term professional learning communities (PLCs) because it best describes a type of community in which teachers learn in order to improve student learning and achievement.

The underpinning goal for professional learning is to increase teachers' expertise or improve their practices so that they might better support student learning. This is true of studies into PLCs (Lai & McNaughton, 2016; Vescio, Ross & Adams, 2008), and also studies into external professional learning, for example Reading Recovery (Timperley et al, 2007). Theoretically, before the professional learning can be effective for students' learning, teachers need to gain new knowledge or a new perspective, make sense of that knowledge, and apply it to practice, either individually or as a team. In this section, Catherine investigates the features of professional learning communities that allow teachers to build new knowledge together, Gina investigates how teachers make sense of different learning, Heather investigates how teachers apply new learning to a different context, and Kim investigates how teachers work together as an effective team.

There is an abundance of evidence that Professional Learning can be effective given the right conditions, including the use of time, external expertise, teacher engagement in learning, challenge of prevailing discourses, participation in a professional community, and active school leadership (Timperley, Wilson, Barrar & Fung, 2007). Similarly PLCs have also been shown to be effective given the right conditions (Vescio et al, 2008). However, what is clear is that participation itself does not necessarily lead to improvements. For all the Lead Teachers, it was important to know the conditions that did lead to improvements in their contexts. Kim's inquiry began with a team already effectively enhancing student achievement; for her, it was important to understand the features of the team that were working, because teams change over time, and without a strong understanding of why a team is effective, it may not be possible to maintain that effectiveness. In the studies by Catherine and Gina, schools had invested a lot of time to set up PLCs, so for both of these Lead Teachers it was important to know how the PLCs were working in their schools. This is very important inquiry given that PLCs have risks as well as potential. Similarly for Heather, schools and the Ministry of Education had invested a lot in training teachers to be Reading Recovery teachers. It was important to know whether this training also supported their work as classroom teachers.

In order to examine what professional learning looks like in context, all the Lead Teachers employed a case study methodological approach (Yin, 2014). Case studies typically involve detailed descriptions of the context, which helps to gain an understanding of how the context and setting influence the way the professional learning is set up and run to improve teaching and learning. All the studies used multiple data collection methods, including interviews, observations of teaching across settings, and observations of meetings. Observations were especially critical for the Gina and Catherine's investigations into PLCs, as there were multiple people involved in PLC meetings and each person made sense of the meetings differently, as Gina found in her study. Similarly, for Kim, each person interacted with different members of the team, so Kim needed to find out how knowledge flowed in the day-to-day interactions that people had.

Because the context of professional learning is so broad, it was important for the Lead Teachers to narrow down which aspect of professional learning they wished to focus on. Having done so, they could then examine the existing relevant literature, and apply that to their own context. For example, Catherine began with the desire to understand whether PLCs were effective in her school. She read the PLC literature to find out what characteristics of effective PLCs were relevant to the kinds of PLCs operating in her school, and then used that to guide her research methods and data collection. Applying the research literature to her school's context confirmed many aspects of the literature but also led to the discovery of an important contextual influence on PLCs—that teachers in her school did not directly critique their colleagues in a PLC. Unlike teachers described in the international literature, the teachers in her study used indirect ways of critiquing others. In this way, the international literature only provided a platform for the investigation; the findings were unique to the particular case study.

The case studies here offer immediate and practical ideas for professional learning designed to improve achievement in the case study schools. Like all good case studies they each give a very rich picture of a very specific context. One limitation of all case studies is that they are, by definition, not as readily generalisable to other contexts. However, these case studies are useful to those teaching in other schools for at least three main reasons. First, it is possible for other schools to learn from these case studies if they are in similar settings, face similar problems, and face similar conditions which led to those problems—for example, many schools with multiple PLCs will face the same issue as Gina did regardless of context. Secondly, because teacher learning is both individual and collaborative, it is useful to consider how professional learning is translated into practice, as Heather did. Thirdly, and most importantly, the case studies provide very useful ideas about inquiry designs and methods that others could use to design and conduct inquiries about the effectiveness of the professional learning in their own particular setting.

Chapter 11 Professional Learning Communities: Properties of effective collaborative inquiry in a primary school setting.

Catherine Biggs

This study was set in a high-decile primary school in an urban area of Auckland. Within this school, Professional Learning Communities (PLCs) had been implemented for 5 years. However, there had been no prior formal investigation into whether teachers within the PLCs had the professional knowledge to ensure PLCs were most effective, and additionally there had been no formal investigation into the efficacy of the PLCs themselves. The extant literature suggested that effective PLCs shared three key characteristics: a clear, shared purpose for the PLC; collaborative analysis and interpretation of data; and data-driven collaborative decision making. The research was driven by two primary research questions:

> *PLCs are designed to improve teaching and learning. Catherine's project was designed to investigate whether PLCs at her school were effective.*

1. To what extent do PLCs at this school exhibit the characteristics of effective collaborative inquiry?

2. What enablers and constraints in effective collaborative inquiry exist at this school?

To answer these questions, I used a qualitative case study design over 6 months to give me a detailed understanding about the current practices and processes for teacher collaboration and learning. The methods used included observations of one syndicate's PLC meetings, questionnaires, interviews, and an analysis of relevant documentation. All data were transcribed and analysed thematically, then triangulated to form a rounded narrative of PLC practice.

Analysis of the PLC documentation indicated that there was a clear, shared purpose for the meetings. During the meetings, participants appeared to have a shared understanding of the purpose, and from the interviews, there was almost uniform agreement across the participants. However, the purpose of each meeting was not explicitly stated. Secondly, observations indicated that there were already effective practices for collaborative data analysis, interpretation, and use of the findings to drive decision-making practices. While there was little evidence of explicit critique and challenge of ideas across participants, there was some evidence that participants were critiquing ideas indirectly. Teachers tended to offer indirect critique masked as a critique of their own ideas, by giving examples of changes to their past practice, or including themselves in the practices they were critiquing. A fundamental ingredient for critical conversations to occur is a strong relational trust across PLC participants. Interviews revealed that while all participants understood the importance of this, there were constraints to the development of trust within the group, which may explain the lack of explicit critique of ideas and decisions during the meetings.

> Catherine's literature review allowed her to develop a frame to investigate the effectiveness of the PLCs using the different data sources.

The PLCs utilised a planning document, which followed a clear inquiry framework using a school action research model. This document guided participants through the inquiry process through a series of leading questions, and such documents could become key enablers to effective processes. However, the evidence also suggested that such documents need to be very carefully developed to ensure that they enable conversations to contain respectful collaborative critique through the analysis, interpretation, and decision-making stages of the discussions.

In sum, the findings suggested that further professional development could have supported teachers to develop skills in professional collaboration and sense-making discussion processes. The findings also suggested that planning documents that are carefully crafted can be a strong enabler to guiding effective PLC conversations.

While the use of observations provided an important lens into these conversations in practice, one drawback of the observation framework was that it only counted explicit statements that were made during the observation. While the use of interviews and questionnaires mediated this issue—as they were intended to do—I would try to incorporate more indirect forms of evidence in such a framework if I were to do this research again.

> Catherine's study identified the strong enabling potential of carefully crafted planning documents. She also identified that teachers were less inclined to explicitly critique one another's ideas than was described in the international literature. She concludes that specialised skills support the effective functioning of PLCs.

Chapter 12 Does Reading Recovery training change the way teachers interact with students in guided reading?

Heather Hardy

Reading Recovery is an effective early literacy intervention designed to reduce the number of children with literacy difficulties in schools. Reading Recovery provides daily one-to-one teaching with a specially trained teacher for children making the slowest progress in literacy learning after a year at school. Teachers undertake a year-long training, working in a collaborative apprenticeship model. This training incorporates teaching as inquiry and employs evidence-based strategies. Reading Recovery was designed by Dame Marie Clay and is a well-researched, proven effective literacy intervention in several countries. Reading Recovery has also been reported to be of benefit to Māori and Pasifika students (McDowall, Boyd, Hodgen, & van Vliet, 2006).

Heather's study arose from previous research which had important implications for her role as a Reading Recovery tutor.

The present study was designed to investigate teachers' learning across different aspects of their practice. Elley (2004) identified that many effective junior classroom teachers of literacy cited Reading

Recovery training as being a factor in their students' success. Thus, the study was designed to understand why trained Reading Recovery teachers might be effective in a classroom setting.

Two questions guided the research:

1. In the Reading Recovery training year, what changes are observed in the teachers' ability to foster and support literacy processing in reading?
2. To what extent might these changes influence their teaching in Reading Recovery and within a guided reading context in the junior classroom?

The study used a mixed method approach and involved three teachers from three different schools in Northland, New Zealand, who were participating in Reading Recovery training and also teaching guided reading in the classroom. Tools used for data collection included participant questionnaires, classroom and Reading Recovery observations, and participant interviews. Observations and participant interviews were audiotaped, coded, and analysed. Although this study was not specifically 'school-level problem solving' it involved two 'communities of learners' as the teachers were part of two Reading Recovery training groups in Northland. The study took place over 4 months with data being collected in May (Phase 1) and September (Phase 2). Comparisons were made between the two points of collection.

Heather used a variety of data sources to gather a rich picture of the teachers across both settings and over the course of the year.

In both Reading Recovery and guided reading observations, teacher moves and interactions were identified, coded, and analysed as to whether they were considered to be facilitative of literacy processing. Across time, teachers changed in the degree to which their teaching moves were focused on facilitating the students' own literacy processing. During Phase 1, teachers displayed fewer facilitative moves (e.g., encouraging children to search for and use information, to reread and confirm or self-correct, or to monitor their reading) than non-facilitative

Heather analysed transcripts of the lessons. She developed a coding frame which sorted all the types of moves made by teachers. She was then able to identify those moves that supported students to solve their own problems.

moves (telling the word, non-specific praise) in total. During Phase 2 this type of interaction had increased from 48% to 58%.

Change was noted in how teachers oriented students to a new text with the promotion of meaning and structure as powerful sources of information, both in Reading Recovery and guided reading settings. One of the teachers had not previously used a book introduction during guided reading even though she was a very experienced junior classroom teacher.

When considering the kinds of information promoted by the teacher during the first reading of a new text, there was a clear shift from promoting mostly visual information to including meaning and structure. This was evident particularly in two out of the three teachers in both Reading Recovery and guided reading observations.

> Heather analysed teachers' interviews to understand how they thought their teaching was changing. She then checked in the observations for evidence of these changes.

Over the course of the study, evidence of how teachers reported that they had changed. Observations also confirmed that teachers displayed an increase in the facilitation of monitoring strategies.

Data showed an increase in the number of prompts fostering monitoring strategies from seven during Phase 1, to 26 during Phase 2 in both settings.

Over time teachers became more succinct with their talk. One teacher clearly reduced the amount of talk to elicit a response from children. The 'longest word-solving episodes' were noted during each phase, with one teacher in particular using her words more economically during Phase 2. She reduced her talk from 65 words to 15 words in order to assist the child in solving a word.

> Teachers developed skills when working with children and for knowing about children.

A further characteristic of change included the promotion of fluency in phrased, fast, and fluent reading. One teacher participant reported: "I've learnt more how to help [students] to be more fluent."

As teachers are individuals, it became apparent that teachers were highlighting different areas of growth. However, some common themes emerged. Teachers stated that they were better able to monitor their students' progress and were able to complete running records quickly.

They knew when to use various prompts and how to use appropriate prompts to strengthen the processing system. One teacher commented on her focus on meaning and structure having changed from a reliance on visual information. Further comments incorporated aspects of attending to child reading behaviour through close observation. Additionally, teachers espoused a growing awareness of their specific use of language when fostering independence in reading processing. These teacher participants were learning to make astute decisions in response to their students' needs encouraging them to become independent problem-solvers. Many of these revelations reflect an understanding of the importance of evidence-based teaching in order to adjust teaching and raise student achievement.

As Reading Recovery is designed as an individual tutoring intervention for struggling readers and writers it would be inappropriate to provide Reading Recovery in a group setting. However, the study supports the notion that expertise in lifting and extending student achievement in early literacy learning can transfer across the settings. This exploration of teacher change during the Reading Recovery training year could explain why previous research has identified Reading Recovery trained teachers as effective classroom teachers.

The small sample size in Heather's study is appropriate for finding out how something might work. It doesn't allow an assumption that it will always work that way.

Overall the findings suggest that teachers in this study demonstrated a growing awareness of how to strengthen students' literacy processing systems both in Reading Recovery individual tutoring sessions as well as in a classroom group situation. Results are discussed in the context of change being a continuous process of teachers learning how to facilitate literacy learning. This study further endorses the value of the Reading Recovery in-service course and has implications for Reading Recovery tutors and national policymakers.

This study of teacher learning provided some evidence that it is possible for teachers to make sense of their learning in such a way that it benefits other aspects of their practice.

Chapter 13 How teacher–leaders make sense of what they learn when they are involved in multiple inquiries

Gina Hemmingsen

This study sought to investigate the structure of professional learning. Teachers at the school were involved in multiple Professional Learning Communities (PLCs), each focused on a different inquiry topic. While the PLCs were intended to follow a similar structure, the topics appeared to teachers to be disconnected. At this stage, the impact of multiple inquiries across multiple PLCs on professional learning groups was not known. Each year, student achievement within the topics of these inquiries improved, which could indicate that the PLC inquiries were successful. However, teachers had reported feeling overworked and this was acknowledged in previous staff surveys.

Gina's study arose out of a concern to evaluate the impact of school professional learning processes on teachers' learning and practice.

As the group of people who were involved in all the school PLCs, teacher–leaders were the focus of the study. At the school, teacher–leaders were involved in at least three different professional learning communities, each of

The sample of participants in Gina's study were selected as 'key informants' ensuring coverage of the issue.

which had a different topic focus; some communities had multiple topics within their community. The priorites for the research were to understand: (a) how multiple topics affected what was learned and how teacher–leaders made sense of that learning; and (b) how PLCs were connected to one another within the professional learning.

> *Gina drew from literature about sense-making, professional learning, professional learning communities, and networked learning communities in order to understand how they might work best.*

Prior studies indicated that professional learning should be connected closely with teachers' daily practice, provide multiple opportunities to learn, and be sustained, intensive, and inquiry based (Timperley, et al., 2007). PLCs that have shared values, that are collectively responsible and focused on student learning, and demonstrate high levels of trust and respect for one another have been shown to improve student achievement (Bolam, McMahon, Stoll & Wallace, 2005).

However, teachers bring their own belief and value systems, prior knowledge, and experiences to each new professional learning context. This means that in order to develop new knowledge and apply it within their practice, teachers need to have a clear understanding of how the new knowledge fits in or differs from their previous practice. Consequently, teachers can have their old and new pedagogies working side by side until they are fully able to enact new ways of teaching or new understandings of how students learn.

A qualitative case study was used to explore how teacher–leaders made sense of their learning in multiple professional learning communities. The study drew from school documentation and interviews. Teacher–leaders' intended learnings were compared with how they made sense of these during one school term. Interviews

> *The research alerted Gina to the need to understand how participants were making sense of the learning in relation to their prior knowledge so that they could apply it in practice.*

were conducted with the teacher–leaders and the principal to ascertain the intended structure and content of their professional learning. Minutes of meetings and documentation relevant to them was triangulated through interviews with the teacher–leader to identify what they actually learned and how they made sense of that learning.

For analysis to take place, data were first coded according to themes. The initial categories were generated through open exploration of the data arising from the interviews. These initial codes were then compared with theory. This process generated initial themes from the interviews which were then checked against meeting minutes. Participants checked the interpretations and clarified misunderstandings.

Case studies are used to explore complex issues that are embedded in a specific context. They are a means of gathering and analysing in detail how something works.

Findings from this process suggested that the teacher–leaders' prior learning and belief systems affected the clarity of their learning. They highlighted the importance of sharing the understanding of what is to be learned and how it is best learned. In the study, competing initiatives confused learning or amalgamated and redirected learning. High co-ordination and trust enabled teacher–leaders to make their learning pathways more coherent across the network of PLCs.

Combined, the findings suggest the importance of formative evaluation of teachers' learning is included in professional learning communities. This would allow members of the community to share their understanding about what is being learned, and improve coherence among the group. Given more time and scope, a future study would survey all staff to see the significance of the teacher-leaders' efforts to co-ordinate the professional learning in school.

Coding reduces the data using a framework to capture the big ideas. The framework might come from previous research (deductive coding), or emerge from the data (inductive coding).

Chapter 14 Features of success: A study of an effective teaching community

Kim Henry with Aaron Wilson

Most of the other studies reported in this book were initiated because the Lead Teachers had identified a problem of learning or teaching that they wanted to understand and solve. This study is different to the others because the question that Kim asked was why her technology department was able to achieve very positive outcomes for students. She hoped that other departments in and beyond the school would benefit from an appreciative study that identified features likely to have helped make the technology department effective.

Kim's study was designed to understand why something was working well, and what features were necessary for sustained future success.

The study was conducted in a large intermediate school in New Zealand (N=1092 students) with a group of nine technology teachers. Formal and informal sources of evidence suggested that students made more accelerated progress in technology learning than students at similar schools. The Indicators of Progression in technology, for example, showed that by the end of Year 8, 83% of students were achieving at or above the expected level despite only 4% having entered Year 7 at those levels.

One of the hypotheses generated by Kim and her colleagues was that the positive outcomes for students might, in part, be the result of technology teachers working together productively as an effective teaching community. Kim therefore sought to identify key features of this teaching community that might reasonably have contributed to positive learning outcomes for students.

> Kim checked the validity of her analyses by checking with the participants whether they agreed with the interpretations.

The study used a mixture of qualitative and quantitative approaches to find out how the team worked together. Measures included questionnaires, interviews, an "interaction log", and observations of a team meeting. An anonymous questionnaire was used to investigate each of the teacher's beliefs about how the group worked together and what the benefits of working together as a teaching community were. An anonymous questionnaire was used as an efficient way of gaining a good overview of all the teachers' perceptions in a way that allowed teachers to be as open and honest as possible. Interviews, which are more time-consuming in terms of data collection, transcription, and analysis, were used with two teachers to provide a more detailed exploration of the questionnaire items from the perspective of one "newcomer" to the group as well as one "experienced hand".

> Kim investigated whether there was any evidence to support her hypothesis (or whether there was evidence against that hypothesis).

The interaction log was a record that each teacher kept over 2 days showing who else in the department they interacted with and what the purpose of that interaction was. Kim used a free computer program called NodeXL to 'map' all the interactions between group members. Each teacher was represented by one circle with arrows between circles showing interactions. The size of each teacher's circle showed how many different interactions he or she had. This was a useful way of visually summarising all the formal and informal interactions the teachers had. Two team meetings—focused on moderating assessments—were recorded, transcribed, and analysed. After Kim had analysed all the data sources and identified key themes, she used another questionnaire to investigate teachers' perceptions of those themes: this participant checking was an important step in making sure she had correctly interpreted teachers' statements and actions.

The multiple sources of data painted a picture of a team of teachers who work together closely and often, and who had a strong sense of identity and shared focus. The four key features of an effective team that Kim's study identified were related to knowledge, social capital, shared activities, and shared artefacts. All four features were closely linked.

> *The diversity of the teaching team, combined with the strong sense of teaching community, appeared as key features of success.*

The first main feature of the team was a strong commitment by group members to work together to ensure the knowledge base they were working from was accurate. They were committed to openly sharing ideas and challenging one another when necessary. They regularly met to discuss teaching approaches, to plan common units of work and assessments, and to moderate marking. As well as testing knowledge within the group, they tested their shared understanding against external sources of knowledge. These external sources included curriculum documents and support materials, external benchmarks (e.g., assessments), and external experts in technology education.

The second feature was that the group displayed high levels of "social capital". Teachers expressed a strong sense of identity as community members and felt very connected to each another. They trusted one another. Teachers indicated that they regularly shared ideas, observed one another teaching, and gave critique and feedback. Teachers in the group varied in age, teaching experience, specialisation, and prior employment history. The team noted this diversity as an enabling factor. One teacher commented, "In order to provide a differentiated curriculum, there needs to be differentiated teachers." Teachers also reported that they valued the leadership capabilities within the group. One team member in particular was identified as a strong leader, described as able to motivate, listen, respond, and encourage others in the group.

The frequency and quality of shared activities was the third key feature of the teaching community. The interaction log showed 220 shared activities amongst team members over 2 days and that almost half of those interactions were related to creating or using community knowledge. Many of these interactions began as informal chats but ended as knowledge exchanges related to teaching and learning in technology.

The fourth key feature of the community was its use of shared artefacts. Artefacts can be physical, linguistic, and symbolic products of social structures (Lave & Wenger, 1991). The artefacts in this technology department included concrete materials they had developed together such as planning documents and assessments but also less tangible artefacts such as the use of department-specific jargon and in-jokes. Together the artefacts contributed to, and were signs of, a department with a clear culture.

It is important to note that Kim did not attempt to establish a causal link between the teaching community and the positive student outcomes; she does not claim that the features that make the team an effective one are the reason why student outcomes were so positive.

Kim concluded her inquiry with a series of recommendations based on what she had found in her study of her technology department. These recommendations include that schools:

- seek to identify, investigate and share the practices of effective teaching communities within their schools
- promote interactions within teams by keeping teams of teachers geographically close together
- keep teams stable so that they have time to develop social capital
- have teams take responsibility for particular student outcomes and to ensure they have high expectations, shared goals, norms, values, and actions related to those outcomes.

> *Kim's four themes might provide a framework for ongoing success of the team. They might also provide other departments and teaching communities with a useful framework for reviewing how they currently work together and how the way they work might be fine-tuned.*

PART 4 FAMILIES AND PARTNERSHIPS

Rebecca Jesson

Relationships between families and schools might be considered an important goal for many schools, underpinned by the principles of the *New Zealand Curriculum* (Ministry of Education, 2007a). It almost goes without saying that what happens at home is important for students' learning generally, and for their success at school in particular. Parent involvement is strongly related to students' achievement at school: students who have parents who are involved with school and engaged with their learning tend to do well at school (Biddulph, Biddulph, & Biddulph, 2003; Brooking, 2007; Epstein, 2009; Jeynes, 2011). The same correlation works in reverse: children who do well at school tend to have parents who are engaged with their learning or involved with their school. This underlying relationship has motivated an interest in home–school partnerships: schools and parents working together in the interests of their child's learning.

Sitting alongside an underlying empirical relationship is a strong theoretical rationale for the people in children's homes and schools to work together. Most studies in the area of home–school partnerships draw on the Ecological Systems theory of development (Bronfenbrenner, 1994). The model is underpinned by the understanding that learners develop through interactions with people, objects, and texts over time; and that this development will vary depending on the learner's current development, the environment that they are interacting with, and what they are learning to do. Bronfenbrenner conceived the interactions as occurring within nested systems. The learner's immediate environments, including school and home, Bronfenbrenner called micro-systems. What happens at home will have an immediate influence on development. So will what happens at school. The relationships between those microsystems are termed the mesosystem. Alignment between these two different contexts is thought to support the learning in both contexts, thereby promoting greater development. Home–school partnership research is concerned with strengthening the relationships between the home and school systems, thus fostering this stronger alignment. That alignment, however, would need to be additive, so that current family and school practices are strengthened, rather than diminished, by that alignment.

The concern to foster additive relationships with parents underpins all three studies in this section. Each of the studies was instigated by a school-perceived need to acknowledge the power of parents for learning. For David and for Sam, the concern was to work with parents to understand how the school might support them to support their child out of school. For David, the focus was reading, for pleasure or leisure, rather than for school. For Sam, the focus was explicitly academic: secondary school mathematics. Both these Lead Teachers sought to understand the best way to do develop a home–school partnership programme, so that the approach could be additive, and supportive. Sharon, on the other hand, was concerned to understand how parents perceived a process already implemented in her school: the IEP process. For Sharon, that process was conceived by the school as a partnership. Sharon needed to know whether families also thought the process was a 'partnership', and whether the process was considered to support the children's learning.

Existing research in the area of parental involvement, parental engagement, and home–school partnerships can provide a frame of reference for understanding the specific issue in each school. For each of the studies, the literature provided direction for what was already known to work and what to look for in the data. But, for each of the studies, the literature review process unearthed a number of conceptual difficulties particular to this issue. When researching home–school partnership research, the phenomenon of interest needs careful defining, and the way different researchers use terms can differ. Parental involvement, for example, is a wide term, encompassing such activities as communication with school, membership of committees and volunteering, as well as direct involvement with school-based activities at home (such as supervising homework), or less direct involvement (such as establishing expectations, conveying aspirations, and reinforcing routines). Each of these activities is likely to influence learning in different ways, and each research study employs the definitions slightly differently. For each of the Lead Teachers, a lot of time was required to sift and sort through all the different definitions, to understand in practical terms what was meant by 'involvement', 'engagement', or 'partnership'.

A second reason to be careful about the phenomenon of interest is to make sure the review aligns with the inquiry at hand. Although there is strong evidence for the relationships between students' achievement and parents' involvement, none of the scholars was studying the level of involvement of parents. Instead, each of the scholars was studying the relationships, or potential relationships, between the school and families. In Bronfenbrenner's terms, the context of interest was not the micro-system of the home, but the mesosystem of the relationships between home and school. This is an important distinction. While there is evidence that parental involvement is related to achievement, and evidence of the importance of close partnerships for students' achievement, the evidence for the success of introducing new home–school partnership programmes is mixed, with variability of effectiveness between programmes (Martin, 2013). But, for David and Sam, improved student learning was exactly what was intended. Sharon's purpose was slightly different. While improved learning for students was intended, and was a focus of her study, the effectiveness of the 'partnership' approach was her phenomenon of interest.

The nature of the studies reviewed also warrants careful attention. Parental involvement research, in many cases, is correlational. Those students who do well at school tend to be the same students whose parents are involved in their learning. This sort of association identifies things that go hand in hand, but may not cause one another. Correlations can be found regularly between things that do not necessarily cause one another; for example, the number of drownings at resorts increases in line with the number of ice-creams sold; children at primary schools with bigger feet tend to read at higher levels. As in these examples, there may be a number of reasons why those children who do well at school tend to be those children whose parents are involved in their learning. Possible explanations might include past parental experience with school, access, entitlement, comfort levels, and pre-existing alignment. None of these explanations suggest that it is the involvement itself that causes school success, rather these explanations would suggest that the same factors that cause school success cause involvement. Moreover, correlations can also be considered in the negative: students who do not do well at school have parents who do not get involved. Again, explanations may be many and can be multi-directional. When considering associations in studies, researchers must bear in mind that correlations can sometimes identify co-occurring 'symptoms' (sore throats might co-occur with runny noses), rather than 'causes'.

An alternative to correlational evidence is experimental evidence. In these studies, researchers have intervened in some way to see whether changing one part of a situation results in changes in another part (they might stop selling ice-creams at resorts, for example, to see whether drownings decrease). This is what studies of home–school partnerships tend to be: interventions implemented to encourage parents, families, and communities to become involved with the school, often based on the underlying belief that this will benefit the students' learning. As discussed, there is not that much evidence that such programmes will impact student achievement directly. However, there is evidence about the features that make home–school partnerships successful, based on positive perceptions, shared understandings, and commitment (Bull et al., 2008). The features of 'successful' initiatives, and 'successful' partnerships provided a frame of reference for all the studies.

As with all texts, research reports are authored by people with particular views or beliefs, and may have hidden assumptions or underlying beliefs. Many studies focus on the practices within families or the practices within schools. Arguably, such studies seek to understand why some students do better than others, locating these differences in the practices of the families, or possibly differences between the practices of the schools. Arguably also, such studies locate the phenomenon as a strength or deficiency of a particular family, or a particular school (Lewis, Kim & Bey, 2011). Other studies purposefully take a more socio-cultural perspective by seeking to understand how differences are structured within the interactions and relationships between the systems, given the different activity structures and ways of participating in both (Cairney, 2000). All the Lead Teachers took the opportunity in their studies to examine the assumptions underlying their study. For Sam and David, this important shift, from teaching families how to support their children, to unpacking the relationships between the two systems, required an examination of how one might go about designing and delivering a partnership approach which drew on the expertise of both groups, resulted in learning for both groups, and considered ways that students might successfully learn to participate in each. Both researchers ended up acknowledging that partnership designed by one partner is inherently impossible, requiring instead a co-designed partnership approach. Both David and Sam sought to embed this understanding into their studies through their 'bespoke' approaches. For Sharon, the partnership focus meant understanding the perspectives of parents and professionals working together to develop and implement IEPs for children, and seeking to understand any power differentials or loss of shared understandings in the process. For all the Lead Teachers, the challenge was to understand how best to work toward a 'partnership' with a systemic learning focus, rather than one-way communication from the school to the family (Harris & Goodall, 2007).

Methodologically, designing a study that in principle requires co-design is, to say the least, challenging. Both Sam and David divided their studies into phases, to gather information about what was happening for the families, before considering how they might engage with them. To incorporate the flexibility needed within the partnership activities, both used a design-based research framework. This approach is most often used when researchers work with teachers to discover what works best for particular students. In the studies in this section, the researchers worked with families, to discover what might work best for particular families with particular circumstances, opportunities, and constraints. The approach is (family) practice led, and needs-based—drawing on research and theory as well as previous experience jointly to solve on-the-ground issues, as well as contribute to systemic understanding. The process was iterative and dialogic—a conversation between the researcher and the family.

Sharon's aim was not to design an intervention, but her methods were similarly dialogic. In a sense, Sharon's study came later in the iterative process, by seeking to understand how something already existing might be working and what might need redesigning so that the process was a partnership. The dialogic nature of research was also reflected in Sharon's study, acknowledging that a true conversation cannot be planned by one partner in that conversation, but is developed by both partners through the conversation process. To embed this understanding into her research design, Sharon drew on the research processes underlying talanoa.

The studies in this section were all designed to contribute to specific challenges facing their schools. However, at the same time, they also contribute to a more general understanding of the area. David's study contributed a framework for thinking about home engagement strategies: strategies that support student access to resources, strategies to support student engagement in activities, and strategies to model valuing the activities. Sam identified that for mathematics particularly, written artefacts were particularly valuable for focusing joint activity, and access to expertise was a necessary condition for success. Sharon's study found that barriers to partnership existed when 'flexibility' was perceived as not following through with commitments, or when children were perceived to be not well understood.

Each of the studies in this section grappled in their own ways with how a researcher, who is coming from a school perspective, might investigate 'partnerships' with parents, in ways that respect the bi-directional nature of the question at hand. Combined, the studies suggest that partnerships relied on incorporating co-design, drawing on the expertise of families to know that the final 'home school partnership' or IEP process might look like. Each found that it took the combined efforts of both partners.

Chapter 15 Empowering parents and improving reading: Investigating an intervention for adolescent readers

David Taylor

The 'problem' at the heart of this research was how to increase the time adolescents spent on recreational reading. There is longitudinal evidence which suggests a strong link between the quantity of recreational reading that adolescents do and their academic performance. There is also evidence that indicates the importance of home support to establish the habits needed to increase the quantity of recreational reading. At the start the evidence of our school community was anecdotal: it seemed that parents were less involved in the academic lives of their children once they were at high school and that there was a large variance in the quantity of reading students did beyond school.

> *David's study arose from a strong belief in the value of recreational reading for both school and for life.*

Designing an intervention that could be completed in the timeframe, constrained enough for the data to be manageable, but which would still yield conclusions that could be used beyond this particular project, required an iterative process. Although at

> *David's intervention needed to be small enough to be possible, but large enough to make a difference for the school.*

times it was frustrating, like any foundation work it needed to be carried out properly for anything built on it to be useful. Discussing the inquiry with experienced researchers, as well as people who could remind you of your original intentions, was invaluable.

My inquiry was problematised by exploring the literature on parental involvement in children's learning. I expected that this involvement would be universally acknowledged as a positive, but the literature was very mixed with competing views on the value of parental involvement. However, the variation in researcher positions led to a stronger understanding of what types of parental involvement were likely to have a positive effect on student outcomes. This led to a more purposeful and informed intervention which tested the theory that parents/caregivers could be empowered to help with adolescents' reading.

> As is common, the research findings of previous studies did not support a simple view. Often, researchers looked at different activities within similar concepts. David read critically to tease out what was common, and where there were differences.

The setting was a decile 7 co-educational public secondary school in suburban Auckland. It was a two-phase study which sought to both better understand how schools and parents can work together to achieve common goals, and to find ways to improve students' recreational reading habits.

> Before designing his programme David used a parental questionnaire to establish what was already happening and compare that to the literature.

To design the programme, it was important to gather baseline data to establish what practices were currently being used within the school community to support reading at home. This was done as a questionnaire at a parent/teacher interview evening. This stage was crucial for considering how the patterns from the research literature did and did not match this particular community. This information was essential for designing an intervention which had a realistic chance of working in this setting. Data from the intervention was then used to answer the research questions and to better understand if, and how, parents/caregivers in this community could be empowered to support the development of children's recreational reading habits.

The first phase of the research surveyed 54 parents of Year 9 students to establish their beliefs, attitudes, and current practices concerning their support for their children's reading. Key findings from this survey were that rates of use for strategies to support reading at home were low. While parents reported that they thought developing reading skills was more important at secondary school, the role of parents in supporting that development had decreased.

David used a design-based research approach which enabled him to solve an educational issue at his school while at the same time contributing to the theory of how to design a home-school partnership for recreational reading.

The second phase was an intervention involving eight families from the same school. The intervention had two important features. First, a framework was developed and used to align reading strategies to the individual requirements of each family. Secondly, participants were involved in co-constructing the intervention they used at home with their child. The second phase collected six different sources of data: pre- and post-intervention questionnaires, research journals, workshop notes, meeting notes, and emails and other correspondence. These were used to form case study narratives which were then coded using a mixture of deductive and inductive analysis.

David's synthesis of the two bodies of research allowed him to use a theoretical framework to structure his approach with parents, and parents' approaches with their young people.

This intervention was informed by two theoretical frames. The first of these was a parental involvement frame which created bespoke, collaborative, and sustained interventions. The second frame used the categories of accessing texts, promoting engagement in texts, and modelling of a positive disposition towards reading, to align reading strategies to the needs of individual participants.

There were three central findings of the intervention. First, the results suggest that parents can be empowered to increase the strategies used at home to help support their children's learning. Secondly, reading habits can be developed. All families made progress towards reaching the goals they set for themselves and five of eight families reached their goal by the end of the 10-week intervention period. This included reluctant readers increasing their volume of, and interest in, reading. All families who completed

David's intervention sought to align home and school by using the expertise of both.

the intervention intended to continue with their focus on reading at home post-intervention. Thirdly, there were also positive benefits for parent and child relationships reported along with positive effects on siblings who were not the focus of the intervention.

The results provide two important frameworks for helping to align school and home practices. These frameworks offer flexibility to be deployed in a wide range of education settings to help schools achieve their goals. Following the programme we were able to establish that students' academic outcomes can be improved if they do more recreational reading. Schools can work with parents and caregivers to give them strategies to support the development of at-home reading habits. The model of intervention that was developed as part of this research inquiry is applicable to many school 'problems'. Its flexibility allows for the theoretical model to inform school change while still allowing for, and responding to, individual school demographics and circumstances.

From this inquiry it has become clear that getting the research design right is essential—it is very easy to have a scope which is far too great to be manageable or which has lost its key focus when narrowed. It is very important to start with a robust, iterative design process which draws on relevant expertise and literature. As part of this, having critical support to help identify your own assumptions is very helpful—unchallenged these assumptions can lead to flaws which will limit the usefulness of any findings. Finally, even though it might be a long process, there is often only one chance to get it right—so even if it is frustrating, following a sound process is essential.

It is easy to have ideas about what might 'work' to help solve a school-level problem. Interventions involve resourcing and as such come with an opportunity cost. If an intervention is going to be carried out it is important that it have every opportunity to succeed. For this to happen, those carrying out the intervention must establish what is already known about the area of inquiry and design the implementation carefully, using sound research practices.

Using a design-based approach, David was able to draw on what was already known about parental involvement and about recreational reading. He was also able to draw on parents' existing expertise as co-designers. In this way, the programme employed was not imposed but was appropriate to the context.

Chapter 16 Developing a home-school partnership to support Year 9 students in mathematics

Sam McNaughton

This study was initiated to begin testing an emerging theory that greater support in mathematics learning at home would help students improve their mathematics test scores. The school had noticed consistent goodwill from parents/whānau as their children began Year 9, but perceived a lack of support with learning at home. This initial theory was formed from anecdotal evidence from teachers, and from observations that students whose achievement was accelerating were perceived to have parents/whānau who were more supportive of learning at home. Teachers assumed that as the majority of students' 'awake' time is spent out of school, out-of-school activities were likely to have an effect on student achievement at school.

Sam noticed a mismatch: that two perceptions seemed counter to one another. Such mismatches can indicate a fruitful avenue for inquiry. More systematic evidence was needed to inquire into the perceived mismatch.

Previous research alerted Sam to possible explanations for the mismatch, which needed to be checked in his own school.

The research literature supported hypotheses that out-of-school factors can account for the vast majority of differences in educational achievement (Colman et al., 1996; Goldhaber & Brewer, 1997). Key findings from similar studies indicated specifically that parental involvement in home-learning is associated with increases in students' academic achievement. However, previous studies also identified parental frustration or embarrassment when attempting to help their children with material they were unfamiliar with (Hoover-Dempsey, Bassler, & Burow, 1995; Hyde, et al., 2006), which can cause a barrier to supported learning at home. Findings from New Zealand indicated that parental engagement changes in type and frequency when students transition into secondary school (Mutch & Collins, 2012), which might—in part—be due to the increasing complexity encountered at secondary school. If so, an intervention focussed on developing and strengthening home–school partnerships during the beginning years of secondary school (i.e., Years 9 and 10) may prevent, or at least mitigate, some of these issues. A review of the literature revealed two key features of *effective* home school partnerships include tailoring the 'intervention' to a families' specific needs, and strong, positive relationships and collaboration between educators and families.

> Observational studies examine factors that already exist that might explain the differences between groups. Care should always be taken before concluding that one thing causes the other. To test whether a change in one leads to a change in the other, an intervention study is needed.

This study took place at a high-decile (decile 7) co-educational state school in Auckland. In order to maintain a clear focus for the research, we restricted our inquiry to Year 9 mathematics students whose initial test scores were lower than expected on entry. Additionally, we restricted our investigation into parental involvement by only looking at interactions and activities that were academic in focus.

> Intervention studies seek to change something for participants, and then investigate whether the changes lead to the desired changes in outcomes.

The study was designed to have two phases. During the initial phase, we used school-entry tests to identify students with lower than expected achievement. We then asked the parents of these students to complete a survey, which was designed to identify their perceptions around their child's learning.

Sam used purposive sampling to target a specific 'population' which might most benefit from his intervention while simultaneously helping him understand the issue in more depth.

Thus, in Phase 2, findings from Phase 1 were used to help inform the development of a *co-constructed, bespoke* intervention to assist parents to help support their child's learning at home. The intervention was based on a 'professional learning communities' model, whereby parents shared their specific issues and strategies, and were given advice, activities, and approaches to trial at home. Each intervention comprised a series of four group workshops with parents, carried out over 11 weeks. Student achievement was monitored using mathematics test achievement data, and parent perceptions were collected via the initial questionnaires, and 'intervention' parents' journals, comments during workshops, and self-reflections. In the initial phase, 60 questionnaires were completed and analysed; from those, six parents agreed to be a part of the intervention programme in Phase 2.

Rather than adopting an existing intervention, Sam designed one that met the needs of his participants.

Results from the Phase 1 questionnaire indicated four key findings. First, parents believe mathematics education to be important, and that their support and involvement in their child's mathematics learning is important for their child's developing maths skills. Secondly, families' perceptions of their own mathematics ability was perceived to be a major barrier, as between 30–45% of parents didn't feel that they had adequate skills to support their children at home. Thirdly, the most common use of non-school based mathematics in the home was to do with money calculations (followed by games and cooking activities), and homework was the largest school-based mathematics activity that took place at home. Lastly, homework was seen as the primary enabling factor for parents to provide support—but the parent's own ability to help was reported as the primary barrier to support.

Parents' views informed the design of the intervention.

Findings from Phase 2 data (including post-questionnaire data, parent journal entries, and comments given during the workshops) indicated that the use of an artefact in the home was a major enabler for focusing the home-based learning. This included formal, structured homework, but also included other artefacts such as notes and workbooks. Additionally, access to 'experts' was found to be another enabler. For example, parents reported success from utilising the expertise of family members, friends, and teachers to help support their child's mathematics learning at home. Additionally, it is important to note that each of these enablers was found to be individually necessary, *but insufficient*, to support students' learning at home. For example, expert help was perceived as less effective without an artefact from which to structure the next steps for learning.

Sam used multiple sources of data to investigate what worked, for whom, and under what conditions.

Following the intervention, parents perceived that the intervention helped build home–school partnerships around learning, and helped to promote positive feelings and enjoyment about learning mathematics—both for themselves and their children. Participants expressed an increased confidence in their own mathematics ability, as well as increased capability in finding and accessing expert support.

Using qualitative data analysis techniques, Sam sorted and categorised the themes that recurred. Sam purposefully sought to understand both barriers and enablers for parents.

In addition to these positive findings, there is evidence to suggest that students' knowledge of algebra increased after the intervention. Prior to the intervention, all students with parents in the intervention group had been identified as "low achieving in mathematics" based on their MidYis test, administered prior to their entry into secondary school. After the intervention, these students all performed well on the school algebra test, with five of the six students receiving an 'achieved' grade (indicating they were performing at expected level), and one student attaining a merit grade (indicating they were performing above expected level). The results arising from this study are sufficiently positive to justify a scalability test for next stage, which is now being funded by the Teacher-led Initiative Fund (TLIF). This grant will enable the intervention to be trialled across three secondary schools in the areas of English and mathematics in 2016–19.

> *Parents' reports showed that Sam's intervention was successful in terms of parents' perceptions of supporting their young people in mathematics. But Sam went beyond looking at changes for participants. Sam's inquiry tested his hypothesis, that parental support would result in gains in student achievement.*

Chapter 17 Understanding parents' perspectives of the IEP process

Sharon Fuemana

Studies have shown that when schools work with parents in partnerships focused on learning, the impact on student achievement and wellbeing is far greater than when schools work alone. This is even more important for students with varied and complex Special Education Needs (SEN) who require specific and additional support to ensure their holistic needs are met in an inclusive mainstream classroom.

Sharon's school needed to understand how well their existing partnerships with parents were functioning from the parents' perspectives.

The IEP (Individualised Education Plan) was introduced as a means of communication between schools and parents, to support parents' rights to be involved with and be consulted about their child's learning. Its intention is to "unite educators, parents, and students in a team effort to achieve an appropriate education for students with disabilities" (Lovitt, Cushing, & Stump, 1994, p. 34). The IEP has been the subject of extensive research for close to half a century but its success and ability to empower parents in championing their children's education has been varied. In addition, the majority of research about the IEP has been discussed from the perspectives of educators; limited research has explored the perspectives of parents, and even less from the perspectives of Pasifika parents. In the study, I aimed to address this gap in research, by examining the perspectives of parents (who were predominantly of Pacific Island descent) of IEP students from a mainstream decile 2 school in Auckland. In this study I used a mixed-methods design to answer three research questions:

> *Sharon designed her research questions to start wider, and then increasingly narrow the focus.*

1. What is the nature of the IEP process?
2. What is a successful IEP process from parents' perspectives?
3. What is a successful IEP process from Pasifika parents' perspectives?

Using talanoa as a Pasifika methodology for the qualitative semi-structured interviews, the study draws on participants' experiences of the IEP process over a 3-year timeframe. In addition, the student achievement data was gathered to enrich the qualitative evidence, particularly on whether the IEP process had impacted on achievement.

This study involved six children who were involved in an IEP intervention in 2012, and all but one of whom continued their IEP programme through to 2014. A total of nine parents of these children also took part (six mothers and three fathers), representing a range of ethnic backgrounds including Pasifika, Māori, NZ European and one Afrikaans parent. Twelve professional participants also took part. As the study took place during 3 years prior, a retrospective lens was used within the mixed-methods design. One advantage of this was that perspectives of the IEP process were not limited to one teacher/facilitator; participants had a range of experiences with a variety of professionals from which to draw conclusions about what a more effective IEP might look like.

The study involved three stages: examination of student's reading achievement and IEP goals across 3 years; and case-study interviews of nine parents, nine professionals and five students. Interviews were then analysed using an inductive approach including open, axial, and selective coding (Strauss & Corbin, 1994).

Qualitative findings showed that all participants believed the core nature of the IEP process is one that is focused solely on the child. As one student put it: "It's all about me. I'm learning." (Student 1). Another strong theme was about developing strong and supportive relationships; parents viewed a successful IEP process involving professionals spending time to get to know the child and the family contexts and backgrounds. Professionals and parents alike particularly expressed a view that understanding and appreciating the culture of the student and their family was of particular importance. Additionally, according to Pasifika parents, successful IEP processes involve consultation including all parties, and a commitment of everyone to fulfil their responsibilities:

> *Sharon needed to understand what 'successful' meant from different perspectives.*

> Making [the child] feel part of the plan, it didn't look like the school said you do it this way but my [child] had an input and we did an agreement thing so everyone agreed to the plan. (Parent 5)

> If you say you're going to do something with our kids, then do it! So long as people do what they say they are going to do and I do what I say I'm going to do ... it should just come together. (Parent 7)

A final key theme was on the IEP document itself, as a current, 'living' document: "It's a living document. It's used, not put away in a cupboard." (Professional 5).

While these findings relate to the aspects of a successful IEP, parents identified some barriers from their experiences, particularly when there was not adequate time spent in consultation between all parties prior to the transition to the IEP process. This often caused parents to feel their child's behaviours were not properly understood, as exemplified in the following comments:

> *Barriers to success were identified when parents felt their child was not well understood.*

> I think what would have helped was if the meeting had happened sooner and the transition period had been longer, so it would have given the teacher more time to get to know him and his little quirks ... Even for her to be able to come back to us and say, "Well I've noticed this and this, so what do you do about it (at home)?" (Parent 3)

The teacher said, "Oh I had a child with (condition), I know what it is" and I thought well, our child's different ... every child's different ... and every case is different. But what we found when he got into the classroom ... the reality of that was very different from what (the teacher) thought.
(Parent 4)

Quantitative findings showed variability in increases in student achievement in reading, with some students making year-on-year progress, while others made gains in one year and losses in another. Overall, students did make progress across the 3 years, although the gains made for some students were small and below national expectations. Of the 40 goals set across all students in the first year, the majority (74%) had been achieved by the third year

The study concluded that while there were some successes, the IEP process is complex and is mostly influenced by the interface of parents and their lived realities, and the ambiguity of the school system which sometimes seemed to support and other times appear to constrain it. Consequently, the collaboration in relationships, while fundamental to the success of the process, may not always equate to responsive consultation, particularly for Pasifika families.

> *Flexibility in school systems operated sometimes as a support for the process and sometimes as a constraint for parents.*

The findings of this study lead to the recommendation that professionals need to fine-tune the process—before, during, and after the meetings. This includes defining the roles and responsibilities of school-based parties, spending time understanding—and valuing—parents' knowledge, beliefs, and involvement, and building on a culturally responsive model of shared learning and understanding.

> *Sharon used the results of the study to fine tune school practices, to overcome identified barriers, and any ambiguity of roles, so that agreements and processes were clear to all and followed through in line with parents' expectations.*

References

Bangert-Drowns, R., Kulik, C., Kulik, J., & Morgan, M. (1991). The instructional effect of feedback in test-like events. *Review of Educational Research, 61*(2), 213–238. doi:10.3102/00346543061002213

Biddulph, F., Biddulph, J., & Biddulph, C. (2003). *The complexity of community and family influences on children's achievement in New Zealand: Best evidence synthesis* (BES). Wellington: Ministry of Education.

Bishop, R. (1998). Freeing ourselves from neo-colonial domination in research: A Maori approach to creating knowledge, *International Journal of Qualitative Studies in Education, 11*(2), 199-219, DOI: 10.1080/095183998236674

Bishop, R., & Berryman, M. (2006). *Culture speaks: Cultural relationships and classroom learning*. Wellington: Huia.

Bishop, R., Berryman, M., & Wearmouth, J. (2014*). Te Kotahitanga: Towards effective education reform for indigenous and other minoritised students.* Wellington: NZCER Press.

Black, P., & Wiliam, D. (1998). *Inside the black box: Raising standards through classroom assessment.* London, UK: King's College London.

Bolam, R., McMahon, A., Stoll, L., Thomas, S., & Wallace, M. (2005). *Creating and sustaining professional learning communities* [Research report number 637]. London, UK: General Teaching Council for England, Department for Education and Skills.

Bronfenbrenner, U. (1994). Ecological models of human development. In T. Husen and T. N. Postlethwaite (Eds.), *International Encyclopaedia of Education* (Vol. 3., 2nd ed., pp. 1643–1647). Oxford, UK: Elsevier.

Brooking, K. (2007). Home–school partnerships. What are they really? *set: Research Information for Teachers, 3*, 14–18.

Bryk, A. S., Gomez, L. M., Grunow, A., & LeMahieu, P. G. (2015). *Learning to improve: How America's schools can get better at getting better.* Cambridge, MA: Harvard Education Press.

Bull, A., Brooking, K., & Campbell, R. (2008). *Successful home–school partnerships*. Wellington: Ministry of Education.

Butler, D., & Winne, P. (1995). Feedback and self-regulated learning: A theoretical synthesis. *Review of Educational Research, 65*(3), 245–281. doi:10.3102/00346543065003245

Cairney, T. H. (2000). Beyond the classroom walls: The rediscovery of the family and community as partners in education. *Educational Review, 52*(2), 163–174.

Clay, M. M. (1991). *Becoming literate: The construction of inner control*. London, UK: Heinemann.

Coleman, J., Campbell, E., Hobson, C., McPartland, J., Mood, A., Weinfeld, F., & Robert York. (1996). *Equality of educational opportunity*. Washington, DC: US Government Printing Office.

Creswell, J. (2013). *Qualitative inquiry and research design* (3rd ed.). Thousand Oaks, CA: Sage.

Elley, W. (2004). Effective reading programmes in the junior school. *set: Research Information for Teachers, 1,* 2–5.

Epstein, J. (2009). *School, family, and community partnerships: Your handbook for action* (3rd ed.). Thousand Oaks, CA: Corwin Press.

Fletcher, J., Parkhill, F., Fa'afoi, A., & O'Regan, B. (2009). Pasifika students: Teachers and parents voice their perceptions of what provides supports and barriers to Pasifika students' achievement in literacy and learning. *Teaching and Teacher education, 25*(1), 24–33.

Goldhaber, D., & Brewer, D. (1997). Why don't schools and teachers seem to matter? Assessing the impact of unobservables on educational productivity. *Journal of Human Resources, 32*(3), 502–523.

Hamilton, R. J., Farruggia, E. R., Peterson, E. R., & Carne, S. (2013). Key competencies in secondary schools: an examination of the factors associated with successful implementation. *Teachers and Curriculum, 13,* 17–55.

Harris, A., & Goodall, J. (2007). Parental involvement and educational attainment. *Education Journal, 101,* 12.

Hattie, J., & Timperley, H. (2007). The power of feedback. *Review of Educational Research, 77*(81), 81–112. doi:10.3102/003465430298487

Hill, J., & Hawk, K. (2000). *Making a difference in the classroom: Effective teaching practice in low decile, multicultural schools*. Auckland: Massey University.

Hipkins, R. (2006). *The nature of the key competencies A background paper*. Wellington: New Zealand Council for Educational Research.

Hoover-Dempsey, K. V., Bassler, O. C., & Burow, R. (1995). Parents' reported involvement in students' homework: Strategies and practices. *Elementary School Journal, 95,* 435–450.

Hyde, J. S., Else-Quest, N. M., Alibali, M. W., Knuth, E., & Romberg, T. (2006). Mathematics in the home: Homework practices and mother-child interactions doing mathematics. *Journal of Mathematical Behavior, 25*, 136–152.

Jesson, R. N., McNaughton, S., & Kolose, T. (2014). Investigating the summer learning effect in low SES schools. *Australian Journal of Language and Literacy, 37*(1), 45-54.

Jeynes, W. H. (2011). *Parental involvement and academic success*. New York, NY: Routledge.

Lai, M. K., & McNaughton, S. (2016). The impact of data use professional development on student achievement. *Teaching and Teacher Education, 60*, 434–443. doi:10.1016/j.tate.2016.07.005

Latham, G., & Locke, E. (2006). Enhancing the benefits and overcoming the pitfalls of goal setting. *Organizational Dynamics, 35*(4), 332–340. doi:10.1016/j.orgdyn.2006.08.008

Lave, J., & Wenger, E. (1991). *Situated learning: Legitimate peripheral participation* (20th ed.). Cambridge, UK: Cambridge University Press.

Lewis, L., Kim, Y. A., & Bey, J. A. (2011). Teaching practices and strategies to involve inner-city parents at home and in the school. *Teaching and Teacher Education: An International Journal of Research and Studies, 27*(1), 221–234.

Lovitt, T., Cushing, S. & Stump, C. (1994). High school students rate their IEPs: Low opinions and lack of ownership. *Intervention in School and Clinic. 30*(1), 34–37.

Martin, A (2013). Family-school partnerships and academic achievement. In J. Hattie & E. Anderman (Eds.), *International guide to student achievement*. (pp 98–100). New York, NY: Routledge.

McDowall, S., Boyd, S., Hodgen, E., & van Vliet, T. (2006). *Reading Recovery in New Zealand: Uptake, implementation, and outcomes, especially in relation to Māori and Pasifika students*. Wellington: New Zealand Council for Educational Research.

McNaughton, S., Lai, M., Jesson, R., & Wilson, A. J. (2013). Evaluation in Effective Research-practice Partnerships. In M. Lai, & S. Kushner (Eds.), *A developmental and negotiated approach to school self-evaluation*. (pp. 73–88). Bingley, UK: Emerald Group Publishing

Marks, H. M., & Louis, K. S. (1999). Teacher empowerment and the capacity for organizational learning. *Educational Administration Quarterly, 35*(5), 707-750.

May, S., Hill, R., & Tiakiwai, S. (2006). *Bilingual education in Aotearoa New Zealand: Key findings from bilingual/immersion education: Indicators of good practice.* Wellington: Ministry of Education. Retrieved from: https://www.educationcounts.govt.nz/publications/schooling/5075

Ministry of Education. (2007a). *The New Zealand curriculum.* Wellington: Learning Media.

Ministry of Education. (2007b). *Pasifika Education Plan: 2008–2012.* Wellington: Author.

Ministry of Education. (2013). *Pasifika Education Plan 2013–2017.* Wellington: Author.

Mutch, C., & Collins, S., (2012) Partners in learning: Schools' engagement with parents, families, and communities in New Zealand. *School Community Journal, 22*(1), 167–187.

Nakhid, C. (2003). "Intercultural" perceptions, academic achievement, and the identifying process of Pacific Islands students in New Zealand schools. *Journal of Negro Education, 72*(3), 297–317. doi:130.216.158.78

Robinson, V. M. J., & Lai, M. K. (2006). *Practitioner research for educators: A guide to improving classrooms and schools.* Thousand Oaks, CA: Corwin Press.

Stoll, L., & Seashore Louis, K. (Eds.). (2007). *Professional learning communities: Divergence, depth and dilemmas.* Berkshire, UK: McGraw-Hill.

Strauss, A., & Corbin, J. (1994). Grounded theory methodology: An overview. In N. K. Denzin & Y. S. Lincoln (Eds.), *Handbook of qualitative research* (pp. 273–285). London, UK: Sage.

Timperley, H., Wilson, A., Barrar, H., & Fung, I. (2007). *Teacher professional learning and development: Best evidence synthesis iteration (BES).* Wellington: Ministry of Education.

Tuafuti, P. & McCaffery, J. (2005). Family and community empowerment through bilingual education. *International Journal of Bilingual Education and Bilingualism, 8*(5), 480–503. doi:10.1080/13670050508668625

Vaioleti, T. M. (2003, April). *Talanoa research methodology: A perspective on Pacific research.* Paper presented at the Power, Politics and Practice—Pasifika Educators Conference, Auckland.

Vaioleti, T. M. (2006). Talanoa research methodology: A developing position on Pacific research. *Waikato Journal of Education, 12,* 21–34. Retrieved from http://researchcommons.waikato.ac.nz/handle/10289/6199

Vescio, V., Ross, D., & Adams, A. (2008). A review of research on the impact of professional learning communities on teaching practice and student learning, *Teaching and Teacher Education, 24*(1), 80–91.

Wenger, E. (1998). *Communities of practice: Learning, meaning, and identity.* Cambridge, UK: Cambridge University Press. doi:10.1017/CBO9780511803932

Wilson, A. & McNaughton, S. (2013) *National Co-ordination and Evaluation of Secondary Literacy Project 2009-2012. Auckland:* Auckland Uniservices. Retrieved from https://www.educationcounts.govt.nz/publications/series/Secondary_Literacy/National_Co-ordination_and_Evaluation_of_SLP

Yin, R. K. (2014). *Case study research: Design and methods.* Los Angeles, CA: Sage

About the authors

Rebecca Jesson is a Senior Lecturer at the Faculty of Education and Social Work at The University of Auckland. She is Associate Director of the Woolf Fisher Research Centre, where she works with teachers and school leaders in New Zealand and the Pacific region to redesign their instructional provision based on research evidence of what is working for their particular context. Rebecca's research interests are in the teaching and learning of literacy, and use of dialogic pedagogies to promote learning.

Aaron Wilson is a senior lecturer in the School of Curriculum and Pedagogy and an Associate Director of the Woolf Fisher Research Centre. His research interests are in interventions to address disparities in education, disciplinary literacy teaching in secondary schools, English, blended learning, and teacher professional development. Aaron led the literacy strand of the Starpath Project and was the Principal Investigator and National Coordinator for the Secondary Literacy Project 2009–11, an intervention in 60 secondary schools that aimed to raise the achievement of underachieving Year 9 and 10 students. Aaron teaches a range of postgraduate courses that foster inquiry skills and knowledge.

Stuart McNaughton is Professor of Education in the Faculty of Education and Social Work at The University of Auckland. His research programme includes work on the development of a psychological model of socialisation (incorporating concepts of teaching, learning and development) applicable to informal and formal educational settings which provides a means of analysing development within and across settings. Associated with this is the demonstration through research applications of ways of incorporating cultural processes in research tools and in explanations of teaching, learning and development. These applications contribute to solutions to a long standing difficulty in developmental and educational psychology, explaining the role of culture in teaching and learning.

Mei Lai is a senior lecturer at the Faculty of Education and Social Work at the University of Auckland, and Associate Director of the Woolf Fisher Research Centre. Mei has led or co-led large-scale projects on improving and sustaining students' literacy achievement across a variety of contexts, from high poverty multi-cultural schools to rural primary and high schools. Mei led a major strand in a national project to build evaluative capability in Government-funded schooling improvement initiatives and a regional intervention to improve reading comprehension and increase the numbers of students gaining national certificates. Mei's research interests are on the use of evidence, through discussion, to support teaching effectiveness.

www.ingramcontent.com/pod-product-compliance
Lightning Source LLC
Chambersburg PA
CBHW080637230426
43663CB00016B/2900